NO
TIGE]
IN
AFRICA!

Recollections and reflections on 25 years of Radharc
by Joseph Dunn

the columba press

the columba press

8 Lower Kilmacud Road, Blackrock, Co Dublin.

First edition 1986
Cover design and typography by Bill Bolger
Drawings by Joseph Dunn
Typesetting by Printset & Design, Dublin
Printed in Ireland by
Criterion Press, Dublin

ISBN 948183 31 4

Dedication

To the Authority and Staff of RTÉ
who never gave us much money.
But who brought us into being,
and gave us good measure in more important things
like friendship, trust and goodwill

Contents

Radharc, if you don't know, is the name of a documentary programme shown on Irish Television. It specialises in the area of religion and is produced by an independent film unit.

Although I direct Radharc films, I never expected to be writing a book about it. Muiris MacConghail, Programme Controller of RTÉ 1 at the time, is to blame. When I reminded him that the Radharc Film Unit would be twenty five years in existence in April 1986, that we were the longest running programme on RTÉ, and that we would soon complete the two hundred and fiftieth film programme, he said: "Write a book about it."

"I couldn't," said I.

"Well all the other freelance film makers have written books." So I had to try.

What emerged, like Gaul, is divided into three parts which can probably be read (or skipped) in any order: 1. How Radharc began; 2. The experience of making programmes in different countries; 3. Some reflections on that experience. It is not, by the way, a book about the philosophy of broadcasting.

It turned out to be a more personal account of Radharc than I originally intended. Not being an accomplished writer, I found I could only write from my own experience; so there are gaps in the story, particularly in the middle years when I was more involved in other things, and the film unit was directed by Des Forristal and managed by Dermod McCarthy.

A friend who read the book in manuscript said that I need to tell something of my background in the Preface.

I am of mongrel ancestry. My mother was quarter English Catholic, quarter Dutch Lutheran, and half Church of Ireland. The Dutchman was the most interesting, being at times a concert violinist, a conductor, and a composer of some two thousand long forgotten works.

My father's family was mostly Irish and Catholic, but his mother rejoiced in the Huguenot name of Boomer or Bulmer. The stock is localised in the Lisburn area. One of them was blacksmith by appointment to William of Orange!

My father was the senior partner in a wholesale/retail fish business which has been in the Dunn family since 1822. He sometimes groaned about money which wasn't unreasonable, because my mother could be extravagant. But by and large we never wanted for much. I have three older sisters, and one younger brother who carries on the business.

I suppose I am what my father used to call ''a jack of all trades and master of none''. I have tried to do a lot of things in life — not all together but in turn.

I have crossed the Atlantic in a sailboat, scuba dived to 200 feet, played football four times a week, completed a course in gliding, designed rockeries, built a pool, painted in oil and watercolour, illustrated magazines, collected tropical shells, (which is easy when one films in the tropics at least once a year), and lots of other enjoyable and foolish things. I hope I may have done a few useful things as well.

Since I was a child, I have been very conscious of the shortness of life and the length (so to speak) of eternity. This drove me towards the priesthood, although very unwillingly. We were not a priestly family and generally I preferred to avoid priests. I prayed hard that the Lord might allow me to lead a normal life, by which I meant college, marriage, a family and successful career. But I never felt my prayers were answered. So the teens were not a particularly happy time for me. I felt much as a young person must feel who contracts leukaemia and has to come to terms with the prospect of early death. Perhaps that is too strong an image, but I can't think of better.

I postponed leaving the lay state by doing an extra year's 'philosophy' at school. But once over the hump and in the seminary, things were not as bad as I feared. Besides, I've never had any tendency to weep over the past or waste time wishing it was different. And so the years to ordination passed quickly.

Since then I have had a happy, fulfilled and relatively untroubled life in the priesthood, which I thank God for. Not all of my priest friends have been so fortunate.

This book, here and there, tells some of the rest of the story.

Hearing the Call

It must have been middle or late May because the apple blossoms were out. We had a day off from school and it was a windless cloudless day, so I did something I didn't usually do — walked up and down the garden saying the breviary.

I was teaching religion twenty-two hours a week in Clogher Road Vocational School, and living as a weekend helper in the Parish of Our Lady of Fatima, Rialto — just around the corner from Mrs Byrne and Gay.

We had a pair of folding doors in the dining room — draughty in winter but a godsend at this time of year. The housekeeper came out and said, "You're wanted on the phone — Archbishop's House."

An unexpected call from Archbishop's House, even in these more relaxed days, is enough to jolt any priest's blood pressure, but in the reign of John Charles McQuaid, of devout and pious memory, such a call from on high was enough to induce cardiac arrest, even in an otherwise healthy young male.

It was the secretary on the phone. "The Archbishop wants to see you." "When?" "This morning. Twelve o'clock." "What about?" I asked, with great temerity. "Something that may interest you." End of conversation.

I didn't have a car. I might have been able to afford a banger, but John Charles didn't approve of priests having cars. There were ways of getting around the rule, but I think I agreed with it anyway so I didn't bother to seek them out. However, this posed problems when it came to visiting Archbishop's House in a hurry. I had a second hand bicycle of uncertain parentage, resprayed some time before I got it in brilliant red, but sturdy, reliable and in p.m.o. — with even a trace of raciness in the curves of the handlebars. I could be at Archbishop's House in half an hour, without losing too much puff. The only problem was that one might as well appear in underclothes as arrive in a lounge suit. No priest was admitted to the archbishop except in formal clothes. That meant a tonsure suit. Now in addition to being very costly a tonsure suit has a number of special features, including tails at the back of sufficient length to get wound around the rear wheel, and thereby improve the braking power of any known bicycle.

So I put on the correct pants (which had no turnups — most unusual for the time!) and the waistcoat, folded the jacket and tails carefully, and put them in the bicycle bag.

From Rialto one of the quickest ways across town is to nip down the canal, through the brewery (where the smell of malt would knock you over betimes) into James's Street, up to Christ Church, and then across the river, Capel St, Dorset St, and in the gates of Archbishop's House.

Fortunately Archbishop's House has a curving driveway with thick shrubs. Pausing for a moment to check that there were no gardeners or visitors around, I nipped behind some laurel bushes, took off my pullover and put on the tonsure jacket.

One of the effects of terror on animals is to increase the rate at which the kidneys secrete fluid. This is a very practical biological mechanism — body weight is cut to a minimum, so no energy is wasted when flight becomes imperative. So I had to have a pee in the bushes before entering the sacred presence.

In the end I never met the Archbishop. Perhaps he was too busy or just changed his mind. I met Fr Liam Martin, his secretary, instead. Nobody was much afraid of him. "The Archbishop's doormat," is how he once referred to himself. "You are being sent on a television course to Manchester; it begins in three weeks' time," he said.

My mind had been working overtime between Rialto and Drumcondra considering the possible reasons for this unexpected and peremptory call to HQ. But I was quite unprepared for this kind of promotion. I had, of course, seen television in other people's houses, but didn't have a set myself. I began to protest unsuitability, but Fr Martin cut me short with some words about holy obedience. In those days holy obedience ended all arguments.

And so began my career in television.

2

2

Learning the Business

Now I suppose many people would be delighted to be sent, expenses paid, on a course in television. And more particularly at that period when everybody knew that television would be coming, and coming soon. But I wasn't one of them. I had planned to become a parish priest.

I think I was also worried about what might be expected of me on the course. If it only meant giving a talk on closed circuit television, or even acting, I thought I'd survive. But if it meant producing ideas, or writing scripts, then I knew I would rapidly be shown up. And I don't like being shown up.

The course was run by ABC, one of the Independent Television Companies based in Manchester. Its purpose was to find new talent for Religious Programmes. The group consisted of English priests of the Roman Catholic persuasion. These were pre Vatican II days when most clergy thought that ecumenics were adequately dealt with by the *Financial Times*.

A similar course had already been organised for Anglican clergymen who included a bishop among their numbers. This course had been rated a success by ABC — most of the newspapers of interest to them had carried photographs of the bishop. One even carried a banner headline, "Anglican Bishop does TV Charm Course". The same bishop was said to have turned to his neighbour one day in the loo and observed philosophically, "this is the only place where I haven't yet been photographed."

I arrived, like Isaac, outside the normal course of events. It appears John Charles had been informed about the course, and

3

asked that I be given a place. ABC (I was told some time after) acceded to the request because there was talk of offering the Irish Television franchise to commercial interests and ABC had hopes that they might be considered. Rightly or wrongly they judged that a word from the Archbishop of Dublin might some day help them in their cause.

The course included, as I guessed it might, a talk to camera by each participant, and an extract from a play in which I played the part of a drunken worker on a picket. During my college days, I had made a speciality of acting in drunk parts, so I became notorious in Manchester as the Irish drunk who (according to himself) had never tasted alcohol.

I hope I am not a nuisance or anything like that.

The course being partly a public relations exercise, food and drink were constantly available. It seemed to me that in this new world of television a hand that wasn't grabbing a microphone or twiddling a knob had to wrap itself around a glass of alcohol. As the week progressed I found it quite intolerable to be the object of interest and pity at every social function because I refused drink. So I gave in, partly to avoid annoyance and embarrassment, and partly because I felt that if I was being thrust into this particular milieu then there was no point in standing out against its traditions and customs. Whatever I may have gained in Manchester, I lost my pioneer pin.

Nobody ever told me why I was chosen to be the first Irish TV priest but I had my own theories. I had appeared in eight or nine plays in Clonliffe and Maynooth, often in a principal part. I had helped to direct the entertainment put on by Maynooth students in their final year. I had medals for debating. I had been resident artist and cartoonist for the student magazine. I used audio visuals in teaching religion in the vocational schools. While I understood these reasons probably led to my promotion (if that's what it was) I didn't feel that they were necessarily the best reasons. It seemed to me after the course in Manchester that television didn't need priest directors, actors or artists. It needed priests who could *write*.

I felt that priests should have a contribution to make to television and particularly in the Irish situation. However, this contribution would be in the realm of ideas. And since ideas in television are best communicated on paper, it is the priest writer who would be in the best position to make a contribution. At the time I had absolutely no confidence in my own ability to write. I didn't know what the diocese expected of me (and I never found out) but if it were to send me for all this training then it might reasonably expect that I would be able to deliver. And not being a writer, I felt essentially inadequate for the task.

I made several lasting friendships in Manchester with people who were afterwards encouraging and helpful. Most importantly perhaps in the realm of ideas, but also in practical ways as well. S E Reynolds, a senior producer in ABC, who directed the course, became a friend. He told me that his people were Orangemen who emigrated from Cork because they found Ireland to be too priest-ridden. He had been in televison since the beginning in Alexandra Palace, was then probably in his early 60s, but still had enormous energy. On the last day of the course he confided with me that he had been asked that day to take charge of the beginnings of ITV in Northern Ireland.

Michael Hollings sat in on the course. At the time he was an adviser to the ITA company with the London Weekend franchise. Afterwards he filled the prestigious post of chaplain to Oxford, and to this day runs one of the most remarkable parishes in England. It's a great pity he was never made a bishop — the Catholic Church in England would be much more interesting today. At one stage indeed it seemed that he might: Bruno Heim, the Apostolic Delegate was heard saying "We must make Michael a bishop". But it never came to be, perhaps for two reasons: the first is probably because no diocese was anxious to have him. When it comes to expressing preferences for a leader in the home diocese, most priests opt for somebody who will not disturb the quiet tenor of their lives. Michael was very demanding of himself and might therefore be demanding of others. The second reason why Michael didn't become a bishop, it is reliably said, was because he informed the Apostolic Delegate that he was aware that his name was being talked about for a bishopric and that before he was appointed he felt the Delegate should be aware of what his policies would be as bishop. The policies were apparently a bit too Christ-like for any human organisation, even a church, to easily accept.

Michael invited me to stay with him in London and attend a meeting of ITA advisers on 20-21 July. I don't remember much about the meeting but I was impressed by Michael. He had had the best education that England can offer. He had earned the Military Cross for bravery. He was thoughtful, intelligent, and had that supreme confidence which is a mark of the British upper classes. I listened a lot. Much of what he had to say about television undoubtedly moulded my own thinking at the time.

Agnellus Andrew, deputy head of Religious Broadcasting in the BBC and the first priest ever to work there, was another of our lecturers. Agnellus is a Scottish Franciscan with a plummy voice who made a mark as a young priest giving sermons and retreats. At a time when Catholic priests were still considered uncouth if not un-British, Agnellus became something of a national figure through his humour, charm and intelligence on a programme called "The Anvil" where he sparred with atheists and agnostics fighting in the cause of God.

After the second world war, the Religious Department in the BBC had thawed enough to consider the possibility of appointing a Catholic priest as an adviser — there already were Anglican priests and ministers of other denominations on the staff. Agnellus was eventually appointed amid opposition. Some time after he was shown a memo from the Director General to Head of Religious Broadcasting (HRB as he is known in the BBC) that on no account must the HRB appoint a Roman priest to his staff. This was dated some months before the appointment. The DG explained to Agnellus later that it was thought a Roman priest would have a divided allegiance and that the appointment would cause great offence to other church bodies. Even as late as 1955 when the decision was made to move him from the rank of adviser to the rank of member of staff, there were strong protests from high Anglican ecclesiastics, and both the *Observer* and the *New Statesman* carried articles complaining about Roman infiltration of the BBC.

There are many stories told of Agnellus and the BBC. The one I like best goes as follows:

The BBC ran a television play which Cardinal Godfrey considered to be a danger to faith and morals. So he summoned Agnellus to his presence to explain why he thought the play was immoral and what he would like to say to the Director General of the BBC. "However, I'm no good at expressing these things, Agnellus. You draft me a letter, and I'll sign it."

So Agnellus duly drafted a letter, which was signed and sent to the BBC.

A good draft, Agnellus, but perhaps a little clerical in style.

A few days later the Director General called Agnellus into his office. "Agnellus, I've had a letter from the Cardinal complaining about that drama last week." Agnellus lifted an eyebrow in mild surprise. "Perhaps we might discuss it between ourselves and you can then draft me a reply." So Agnellus wrote another letter in answer to the first, which the Director General duly signed and sent to the Cardinal.

I think part of the reason why I like that story is because it helps to illustrate one aspect of a priest's life in television — explaining one side to the other.

Agnellus asked me at Manchester to visit his house, St Gabriel's, at Hatch End, outside London, and I went there that summer — the first of many visits.

St Gabriel's is still alive and well, but for me its heyday was in the sixties when Agnellus was host in residence. He had a large house with many guest rooms and anybody involved in broadcasting was welcome to stay.

There was an open table every evening and a wide range of people involved in British broadcasting were either invited or just seemed to feel that they were welcome to come. The food was plain, the drink, flat English beer. But for anybody interested in broadcasting the conversation was superb. The meal was only for openers; after a visit to the chapel — obligatory even for atheists — the crowd wended its way to a very large drawing room with a roaring fire and plenty of whiskey on the piano. After that one just needed stamina. People drifted away after midnight with the last little group turning in about four o'clock in the morning.

Agnellus Andrew introduced me to many people in British broadcasting, people who were not only pleasant to know, but who could be, and at times were of considerable assistance.

Some of the more notable people I met at Hatch End included Hugh Greene and Charles Curran, Directors General of the BBC, Hugh Wheldon, Managing Director TV, Howard Newby, Director of Programmes, Radio, Kenneth Lamb, Head of Religious Programmes, later Secretary of the BBC, Grace Windham — Goldie, Head of TV Talks and Current Affairs, who started *Panorama* and a host of other programmes. Agnellus once called her the brood mare of a number of outstanding BBC personalities, including Alisdair Milne, the present Director General.

3

Study in America

After the course in England I wrote to the Archbishop. I said that I had enjoyed the course, learned a lot, but obviously many aspects of television could only be touched upon in a week.

From what I had learned and heard however I was convinced that the kind of priest who would most likely be able to make a contribution to television would be someone with writing ability. Ideas were relatively useless unless they could be expressed well on paper. And whereas priests were not likely to be running around with cameras and tape recorders, they could present programme ideas and possibly write as well as anybody else. So that if somebody were to be sent for further study, it should be somebody with writing ability. And if I was asked to propose somebody I would propose Desmond Forristal.

And so in early September 1959, with less than two week's notice, Des Forristal *and* I were informed that we had been booked into a three-month course at the Academy of Broadcasting Arts, New York, and that the New York diocese had been asked to find us some place to stay.

We flew in a Super Constellation. The flight was memorable for the magnificent display of Aurora Borealis — light falling in slow motion like a curtain of water over the edge of a high cliff — and for the torture of being couped up for over fifteen hours without legroom in a tiny seat.

We arrived in New York with $1,245 from the Dublin Archdiocese to meet all expenses. After paying our fees we had less than $520. When we went to the Chancery Office in New

York nobody had heard of us. They recommended us to stay at Leo House, a hostel run by nuns for priests. Our expense money from the Dublin Diocese wouldn't have paid for a bed there until the end of the course, not to mention getting something to eat. And it wasn't clear that the diocese of New York was going to put itself out very much for two wandering Irish priests! So we had to be careful. We arrived on the 15th of September. I noted at the end of the month that my expenses which included all food, subway tickets, reading and writing materials — everything for a 15 day period, were 45 dollars and 20 cents.

We ate most of the time in a fast food place called Horn and Hardart. Lunch consisted of brussel sprouts and French fries. We always called them chips and had to be corrected by the lady who served them. This main course was rounded off by a piece of pie; it might be apple pie or pumpkin pie or even blueberry pie — whichever was the day's special. If you *chose* a pie you paid twenty cents or more but the day's special was only fifteen.

I remember wandering down Broadway one night and being met by a gentleman — the kind that people seem to call "bums" in old American films. He told me his recent life story and in particular about how little nourishment of the solid kind that he had been able to partake of that day. I listened with that sympathy and understanding which can only be found in a fellow sufferer. And when he bared his soul, I bared mine. I must have been more eloquent than I intended, because he insisted that I take a coin — slipped it into my breast pocket and would hear no protest.

The course in New York was full time, six hours a day. The policy of the school was to use lecturers who were actively engaged in broadcasting. This policy had obvious disadvantages in an industry where one can be furiously busy one month and have leisure to read the *New York Times* from cover to cover the next. The schedule had to be flexible therefore, and instructors sometimes disappeared for long periods. However, on balance, the situation had obvious advantages not to be outweighed: lectures were related to real and current experience so nobody could throw up the usual criticism of educational institutions, that "those who can, do, and those who can't, teach."

There were six other students taking the course besides ourselves, ranging in age between nineteen and fifty — one Jew, one Black, two Catholics and two Wasps. The Black hoped to be a producer. I remember one of the instructors telling us that because he was black his chances of ever reaching that eminence were precisely nil.

At the end of the course we each had to direct a short play with real actors.

The actors were a sad group. Getting ordered around by a neophyte director in a TV school production was an admission to themselves and others that they needed money and couldn't find a better way of getting it. Their ignominy and frustration surfaced in flashes of temper between bouts of quiet depression.

Seven of us chose dramas from the school files. Des Forristal wrote his own.

After several weeks of badgering the New York Chancery, Des and I were eventually given accommodation in St Agnes's rectory on 43rd Street between Grand Central Station and the UN.

St Agnes's itself was a bit like a railway station. It was a parish but few if any lived in the parish. So what was needed was something to cater for the passing trade. If the pastor could have found more priests he would have had Mass, Communion and Confession going on all day. As it was he had converted storerooms at the back of the school into comfortable but claustrophobic flats, with bathrooms, air conditioning and TV. In addition to the officially appointed curates, he had at the time an Italian priest who spoke little English and a Korean priest whose English was hard to understand. But their orders were valid, and that was all anyone seemed to mind.

Des and I offered Mass, heard Confessions and distributed Holy Communion between 7 and 8.30 each morning; then a quick breakfast and off to school. On Saturdays there were four hours of Confessions (in periods of half an hour or an hour) in addition to parish calls. All Sunday morning was spent in church.

11

He's great! Doesn't understand a word!

The pastor, Monsignor Aloysius P Dineen was of Irish ancestry. He had been chaplain to a famous regiment, the Fighting 69th. The high point of his year was the 17th March when he stepped out at the head of his Regiment in the St Patrick's Day procession, though when we knew him those days were nearing their end. He was considered the toughest parish priest in the New York diocese if not in all America.

In the period where the obedient acceptance by a priest of any appointment at the hand of the bishop was everything, it was not considered a black mark in the diocese of New York to ask for a change from St Agnes's. In the seven years prior to our stay with Monsignor Dineen, he had had a succession of thirty-seven officially appointed curates who had requested transfers.

When we arrived Monsignor Dineen showed us personally around the church and presbytery. He was particularly proud of two things in the church. One was the statue of the Curé d'Ars, which he had dressed in lace surplice and black silk biretta (a four-cornered hat with three peaks that priests used to wear in those days). The other was a large picture — very large — of the Last Supper, a copy of Leonardo's well known painting in Milan. This was executed in strong primary colours, principally blue and red, and stretched the full width of the apse. The Monsignor told us proudly, and with no hint of irony or sarcasm, that many people thought it better than the original.

We also admired a full length portrait of the Monsignor himself. This had been executed at his request with a background of Manhattan Island and the subtitle "Monsignor Aloysius P Dineen,

PP, PA at the gateway of the world''. There seemed to be rather a lot of these paintings around, or copies of same, and at a later date I decided to count them. Between the school, the church, and the presbytery, which were all in the one block, there were twenty-two portraits of Monsignor Dineen ''at the gateway of the world.''

Lunch and dinner at St Agnes's rectory were at fixed times. A bell rang which was a signal for the staff — senior and junior curates and such extras as ourselves — to line up outside the dining room. The parish priest arrived about five minutes later and entered the room, leaving the door open for the rest to follow. Anyone who was late, went out to dine at a restaurant. The door from the dining room into the kitchen had a brass plate 3ft x 1ft on which was written in large black letters with red capitals NO ADMITTANCE.

It was forbidden even to *talk* to the housekeepers! One afternoon at lunch I gave a hurried whispered message to one of the ladies serving lunch only to be interrupted by a loud voice from the top of the table, ''There'll be no talking to the servants. We must have order here.''

On weekdays the parish priest rarely left his room except for meals so we didn't see much of him. But he wasn't idle. Every day at least two neatly typed foolscap sheets appeared on the notice board in the sacristy. These indicated the duty of every priest for every half hour of the day. One checked every night to see what was in store. 7.00 am Confession, 7.30 Mass, 8.00 Confessions, 8.20 Help with Communion, and so on. Monsignor also wrote the Sunday sermon which the curates were instructed to read from the pulpit. The sermons were usually about America as the promised land and Americans as the chosen people or otherwise about some impending collection. I remember reading one of these appeals on a Sunday with the Monsignor below. Afterwards he gave out to me for not reading his words with sufficient conviction.

On another occasion one Sunday when the church was full, I had nothing to do between two sessions of helping with distribution of Holy Communion. So I thought it might be good for me and perhaps, dare I say, give good example to others, if I said a few prayers in the church rather than try and kill time in the sacristy. During Mass the Monsignor noticed me to the side in a row near the front. ''What are you doing there?'' he bellowed in stentorian tones. I don't know whether he heard or even waited for a reply. ''Go into the sacristy,'' he said, ''we don't do that here.''

13

Sunday was a big day for the Monsignor. He attended the later Masses sitting or kneeling at the prie-dieu in the sanctuary, which was decorated with the Latin motto, "Ecce Sacerdos Magnus," usually translated as, "Behold a great priest". This prie-dieu was equipped with a microphone which enabled the Monsignor to shout down the choir and everybody else in church, particularly when they sang "The star spangled banner", the Monsignor's favourite hymn.

The public address system had two speakers outside the church which enabled the Monsignor to sing to a wider audience on 43rd Street. I have since seen and heard speakers on mosques in Indonesia and elsewhere, but it was then, and still is uncommon in the Catholic tradition.

Up at half six, a full day at school, and homework at night. Heavy schedules of Confessions, Masses on Sunday, meant that we had little rest or respite. So when it came to Thanksgiving we thought it would be nice to get a break and perhaps visit some relatives of Des Forristal who lived in New England. So we asked one of the curates and were informed that the correct procedure was to write to the PP — even though we sat every day with him at table! So Des wrote a letter saying that we would like to take two days off and giving the reasons. This was duly delivered in the letter box in the door to the parish priest's office. After a day or two Des's letter appeared on the notice board in the sacristy, and scrawled across it were the words, "any comments?"

Do you think he will let you go?

That morning Des arrived in the sacristy to find an altar boy, about ten years old, reading his letter. The altar boy turned to him and piped up, "Do you think he'll let you go?" Des said nothing. But judging by the colour of his face as he went out to say Mass, it was probably best that he hadn't.

One of the benefits of being a student of television was the opportunity to sit in on television production in many studios around New York. But for me in the end, the most important practical session was a day spent with a film unit on location. This was a professional crew with an experienced director. I expected to be impressed with the clarity of the director's concept and the skill and coordination whereby the crew turned it into useful footage. The day started with a twenty-minute interview on film. When the camera was switched off, the director hummed and hawed for a while and said he didn't think it was what he wanted. And so we muddled through the day, I becoming more and more amazed — and just a little elated. If this was the way professionals made film, then I felt I could do it as well if not better.

I can't say for certain, but the germ of the idea of Radharc probably first came to life that day.

4

The first film

After New Year 1960, Des Forristal returned to a curacy in Halston St. and I went to the new post in University College, Dublin as chaplain.

Now universities have long holidays.

I had a friend, Jim Roche, who produced advertising filmlets and had his own cine camera and tripod. He generously loaned it to me. A classmate of mine in the diocese, Fr Con O'Keeffe, had relatives in Annagry, Co Donegal, and he suggested that we make a film there on the customs associated with St Brigid's Day, Lá 'le Bríde. It was fun planning at a distance but when the time came to film, we felt differently. But for the fact that people were ready and waiting for us to appear with cameras and lights, we might have cancelled the trip and returned to Dublin.

It's a feeling I was to experience many times since and to some extent to this day. Starting a film is one of the more daunting things in life. There are so many decisions to be made and most of them have to be made under pressure. There is the further pressure of working in documentary with busy people, most of whom are under other kinds of pressure themselves.

Lá 'le Bríde turned out to be a ten-minute film. The locals who took part expected it to take about ten minutes to make. It took something more like ten hours. This is something I still hate about film making — it can't be done without putting people who cooperate to great inconvenience.

In this respect, Con O'Keeffe showed talents in addition to research. His good humour helped to jolly along people who agreed

16

to help with the filming, but who didn't expect to be sitting around waiting for the next shot six hours later.

Being a natural pessimist I expected the film to be either wrongly exposed, scratched or damaged in development. But when the picture came back and looked reasonably presentable we both felt a certain satisfaction which I felt could become addictive.

When it was stuck together, polished up and equipped with commentary, we entered it in a competition run by the National Film Institute. Partly because it was shot in the Gaeltacht area, and mostly because we thought we'd stand a better chance of a prize, we entered it in the Irish section and won. This was a further step in my education in film and perhaps finally convinced me that one didn't need any special genius to produce film adequate for television.

Now for the next shot everyone runs around the house four times.

5

A memorandum to the Archbishop

In the Spring of 1961 we were promised an Irish Television Service before the end of the year.

There was little or no talk of religious television and probably less thought about it. Des and I had been doing some thinking and talking about it with some of our friends.

In April that year, I took my courage in my hands and sent the following memorandum to the Archbishop. It summed up our thinking at the time about religion on television, and so I print it without emendation or abbreviation:

SOME PROBLEMS FOR RELIGIOUS TV IN IRELAND

Religious programmes are not sponsored. They cost money but do not earn any. They generally draw a lower audience than any other type of programme. They are undertaken by TV companies as a public service, or at worst to build up a public image of responsibility and integrity.

For these reasons they usually are confined to "valley" periods when audiences are small. They must also exist on a comparatively small budget.

These factors become more significant in the circumstances of Irish TV which will be confined to low budget programmes in every field and which has to compete with ITV and the BBC where financial considerations seem relatively unimportant.

It does not appear therefore that religious programmes can hope for more than minimal facilities. Nor does it seem that they can count on prime time — particularly when one takes into account the competition of other channels. No programme planner can afford to put anything but the most attractive programmes into peak viewing periods because the audience he loses invariably turn to another channel where they stay for the evening. Thus if a programme does not hold an audience, this fact has a large influence on the size of the audience for the programmes that follow. This is not just a sentimental consideration but a matter of hard cash because advertising rates are governed by the estimated number of viewers.

The subject matter of religious programmes, dealing basically with abstract ideas which often do not permit of obvious visual representation, is not a "natural" for TV as for instance is sport or even the physical sciences.

Most people view TV for entertainment. That is a first principle. That is not to say that they are positively opposed to being instructed at the same time — provided the instruction is entertaining. However, it must be remembered that of English homes which can receive both ITV and BBC, three quarters on the average will be at one time tuned to ITV where the greater stress is on pure entertainment and where intellectual content of programmes is relatively lower.

The nature of one's audience must also be considered. By far the majority of viewers, and by far the most persistent viewers, consists of those whose education ceased at the primary level.

One of the basic ingredients of TV is conflict. A difference of opinion is useful. Best of all is a good row — then one can be sure that the viewer is glued to the screen. From this point of view the situation in England presents some advantages with respect to Ireland where the vast majority are in agreement on fundamentals. Archbishop Heenan would find it very much more difficult to make the same impact here where there is no protestant majority with which he could cut and thrust.

Taking into account these problems, and particularly the make up of the average TV audience, the question arises: what is the best programme format to reach and hold a large audience, and at the same time offer them something more than entertainment?

I am of the opinion that there is one format which makes possible serious content and popular appeal. This is the magazine format. The best example of this on the BBC is the programme *Tonight*.

A religious magazine programme would have the following advantages:

1. It would have something for everybody. Viewers will sit through what they consider dull parts of the programme in

19

the hope that the next item may interest them. The programme therefore has a greater hold on its audience — provided of course the items are on the average entertaining.

2. It can have the merit of being topical. Any subject can in fact be made topical with a little ingenuity: "Today is the feast of Brendan the Navigator. Seven centuries ago one of the best sellers all over Europe was a book called The Voyages of St Brendan . . ."

3. It can leave out the boring bits. While we were in America Fr Forristal and I viewed the networked programme, *The Catholic Hour* (actually a half-hour programme). During our stay three series were produced, viz. the Mass, the Bible and American Catholic history. Whilst these programmes were well produced, we found them interesting only in part. The series on the Mass for instance set out to give a logically ordered exposition of the history and theology of the Mass. This meant treating of aspects which did not, and probably could not make good TV. The advantage of a magazine programme, on the other hand, is that one is not obliged to a consistent or full treatment. Take the history of the Mass for example. One could possibly do an interesting item lasting for ten minutes on the Mass in the time of Justin, *(The Catholic Hour* in fact did this) without at the same time having to continue the story up to this day.

4. To get viewers to watch items with really serious content it may be necessary to sugar the pill. By this I mean introduce items of quasi religious or humorous nature. This could be done with brief items in a magazine programme but hardly in another format.

5. Viewers like to see familiar faces. Whether one likes it or not, the personality cult is very important in TV. By having a comparatively small regular panel, the programme *Tonight* has proved that this is possible without monotony.

6. Combined with other programmes, it matters little in a magazine programme whether you tune in late or miss part of the middle.

7. Lastly it is safer. Not every item in the magazine can be a dud whereas a half hour devoted to one subject only, can.

Even if one accepts the fact in theory that a magazine format would seem to be suitable for religious programmes, the fact that it has not been adopted elsewhere (to my knowledge) suggests that there are certain difficulties.

The chief difficulty lies in the fact that this particular format depends heavily on filmed items, interspersed of course with interviews and short discussions in the studio.

Roundabout, the UTV magazine, does not in fact use much film material. This is one of the reasons why it is a dull programme.

There is one very big problem where film is concerned and that is expense. Film stock itself is not cheap, equipment is costly enough, but the overriding factor is the cost of highly skilled labour. The recent film for Bord na Móna cost, I believe, between four and five thousand pounds. The actual film stock used probably did not cost more than a hundred pounds. A supreme example of this was a one minute beer commercial made for American TV which cost $20,000. Film editors in America, we were told, get $15 per hour.

When one takes into account (1) the cost of film stock, (2) the relative scarcity of trained technicians in this country where there has been no film industry worth talking about, it seems clear that production of material for TV on film must be strictly limited. Indeed Mr Roth has stated this publicly.

I see little hope therefore of having more than very occasional use of film facilities for religious programmes, no matter what form they take, unless there was some way for the Church authorities to provide their own.

This would not be completely without precedent. The Radio and TV Apostolate of the Archdiocese of Boston employs a wholetime film cameraman who produces a certain amount of TV material. The French Dominicans have also a film unit which produces material for TV though I have no precise information on the scope of their work. This group produced the two well known films on Holy Week which have been extensively shown in this country.

On the face of it, the practicality of forming a film unit which could produce good film material for religious TV in this country at a reasonable cost seems precisely nil. However the idea is so attractive, particularly in the circumstances of Irish TV, that I feel it is worthy of examination.

While there are many imponderables and suppositions in what follows, I hope I will be excused when I say that I am deeply conscious of this and yet still think that the ideas are worth presenting. What it amounts to briefly is that a film unit could be formed with priests.

21

Film unit
Equipment. As a working estimate this equipment might cost between £3,000 and £6,000.

Film stock. There seems no reason why the cost of film and processing should not be borne by the TV station itself.

Personnel. There does not seem to be any reason either why priests could not make good film technicians provided they have some training and experience. The Columban Fathers for instance have several priests trained already. A Fr G Smith, with whom I am acquainted, was sent to the US last year to study film techniques. For the last three months he has been making films in South America. I surmise that it is hoped that he might make some contribution to Irish TV. He expects to be home soon.

The number required to form a film unit would depend on the scope and volume of the work undertaken. An estimate might be a minimum of four and a maximum of six. Two, possibly three, might require specialist training. (There is a reputable school of film techniques in London). A man like Fr Smith, supposing he was available, would of course have had this training.

Supposing one were to accept the idea of forming a film unit in principle, it would seem foolhardy to buy professional equipment or train men until one had reasonable confidence that such a venture might succeed. However, I think it would be possible to test the idea without any commitment.

Because we did not in fact learn much about film in New York, and because film plays such an important part in TV, a few of us decided to try our hand at amateur film making last summer. Since then we have made a few films and collected some equipment. With a few other items, (two of which are on order for about six months but should be available soon) it should be possible to attempt most of the kinds of subjects that appear on TV. Whereas this material may not reach fully professional quality, particularly as regards sound, it would certainly enable one to provide conclusive proof of the feasibility or otherwise of a film unit.

The official sanction required to test the idea would consist in the release of certain priests from their duties for a period of say six weeks or two months, preferably the latter. Those who might be concerned are as follows:

Donal Flavin, CC, High St. Father Flavin has had some experience of amateur photography and has always been interested in electronics. He is clever at improvisation and has the reputation of being able to fix anything. In a film unit he could take charge of sound recording and/or lighting and exposure.

Fr Forristal, CC, Halston St. His primary work would be scriptwriting. This might entail guiding others with writing talents and ideas.

Fr William Fitzgerald, now in Rome. He has some experience of amateur film making. He also has artistic judgement and considerable ability to get things done. He could make a good cameraman, and/or film editor or director.

Peter Lemass, Chaplain, Lakelands Convent. Fr Lemass is not interested in technical matters. However, he has good ideas and could produce script material. He is intelligent and photographs well and might therefore make a good interviewer on camera.

Cornelius O'Keeffe, Killarney St. Fr O'Keeffe has enthusiasm, a good knack for spotting material and considerable writing ability of an undisciplined type. He is also good at managing people.

Fr Flavin and Fr Forristal would need to be completely released of their duties for the period. As the University would be closed, Fr Dunn would have no positive commitments apart from morning Mass. Some arrangement could be made whereby this could be supplied if and when necessary. The same would be true of Fr Lemass. A private arrangement could be made with a priest friend if and when he had to be absent from the Brugh. Fr Fitzgerald might be on holidays after returning from Rome. Fr O'Keeffe could possibly make a useful contribution without release.

The group might operate somewhat as follows: The Chaplaincy, being comparatively quiet during the summer months, could provide a centre. A meeting would be held most mornings where new ideas, suggested perhaps by an item in the newspaper, could be brought up and discussed. After decisions are taken the group would split up. One perhaps to prepare a script, one to edit new film, two to film some background material.

The group would be prepared to finance the project themselves. This might have advantages as one could say one had no official backing.

Supposing it was determined to go ahead with this pilot scheme, a period of a month, or more likely six weeks, would be necessary to order and receive delivery of film stock and one or two pieces of equipment.

Conclusion

It must be stressed that to undertake the pilot scheme does not commit anybody to anything. Only after the period of trial can the matter be decided.

Many people would not give such a project much chance of succeeding. Even so I respectfully suggest that it might be worth a trial. Firstly because the stakes are high and worth a gamble, even at long odds. Secondly because the experience gained by many people (apart from the group) should be useful when TV starts. Thirdly because the least one can hope to gain might be in itself worthwhile, that is the beginnings of a file on subject matter suitable for TV.

I met John Charles later to discuss this memo. He told us to go ahead, not to worry about failure, and offered £300 towards meeting the expenses.

6

Life with J.C. McQuaid

Between April 1961 when I wrote this memo, and 1972 when he retired, I had a lot of dealings with Archbishop John Charles McQuaid. I became fond of him. I got on well with him, relatively speaking and judging by some of the stories that other priests tell. I'm also grateful to him because I owe him a lot. That said, I must also say that there was no man that I feared more. He exercised absolute power over his priests which nobody in their right mind would dare question. The theology we were taught placed the bishop as pastor of the diocese and priests purely as extra arms and mouths and legs of the bishop. If it were possible to have clones of the bishop, then priests would be unnecessary. The bishop received his mission as a successor of the apostles directly from Christ. To question a bishop's ruling was to question Christ. Perhaps the theology books didn't go quite that far, but certainly that was the conclusion which underlay a lot of the practice.

Then as now, providing he avoids questioning the authority of Rome — particularly on current hot issues which today would be birth control, divorce, married clergy and the ordination of women — the bishop can do pretty well what he likes in his own diocese. Certainly no other bishop can control him.

Nowadays priests are more willing to argue with their bishop, and may even at times rebel, and this, of course, can be a control. Nowadays too journalists feel free to criticise bishops much as they would any other public figure. But both of these are new developments and didn't count for much in the reign of John Charles.

So when I was a young priest in the sixties nothing could be done by a priest in Dublin diocese unless it had John Charles' express support or escaped his notice until it was too late. Little did escape his notice.

The successful priest made John Charles the patron of his enterprise, kept him fully informed, and attributed all success to him. This led to sychophancy of a kind that I found most distasteful in others but which I felt forced at times to practise myself.

As I write this I think of the repetition of a phrase in a speech being made by a priest (afterwards a bishop) welcoming John Charles to a function: "And as your Grace most wisely said . . ."

It's easy to be critical of this attitude, until one remembers that one careless move might mean that a life's work could be undone. One priest whom I admired had put many years of hard work into building up a boys' club. He had the rashness to suggest to John Charles in some undiplomatic way that the scope of the work might justify a fulltime priest chaplain. Two weeks later he got another appointment at the very end of the diocese, in a parish where he could find little real work to absorb him. So he took up golf.

In the beginning we needed John Charles' approval for priests to work at television, even if, as was usually the case, their work was done during their annual holidays and at their own expense. We needed to build up trust so that we could continue to work with minimal interference.

I received a peremptory reminder early on of the need to keep him informed, and ask permission where possible:

9.3.62

Dear Father Dunn,
I understand that you attended a Congress at Monaco. May I ask by whose permission did you leave the diocese?
I am,
Yours sincerely,
✠ John C McQuaid
Archbishop of Dublin.

This Congress was a meeting of the International Catholic Organisation for Radio and Television.

In my reply I made the following points:
Des Forristal and I were asked to attend the Congress by the Catholic Television Interim Committee (a body appointed by the

26

Hierarchy, and chaired by John Charles' representative).

We were asked to go on the 31st of January which left three days to make arrangements. Des Forristal had called at Holy Cross College to see the Archbishop's Radio & TV representative, Canon McCarthy, but he was in bed with influenza. Des then wrote on our behalf to Canon McCarthy informing him of the position and asking for a letter of credence. We had then secured celebrets* from the Vicar General.

I continued, "Having taken these steps, and bearing in mind the letter to me from the secretary of the Television Interim Committee of November 13, 1961, stating that Your Grace was very willing that we should make ourselves available to the committee to help with arrangements for religious programming, we judged that it was not necessary to trouble Your Grace personally for permission."
I remain,
My Lord Archbishop,
Your Grace's Obedient Servant,
Joseph Dunn.

(This was the way we had been instructed before ordination to end all letters to the Archbishop.)

The reply came dated 12th March:

Dear Fr Dunn,
I thank you for your letter.
The Vicar General had explained to me his belief that you, in asking for a celebret,* must have already asked my permission to leave the diocese.
I am,
Yours sincerely,
✠ John C McQuaid
Archbishop of Dublin.

And so the matter rested.

As far as my memory and records go John Charles only ever suggested two subjects for programmes. One of them we were already doing, the other we conveniently forgot about. His only recorded comment on a programme is dated 20.10.69:

*A document to say the named person is a priest in good standing who might be given facilities to offer Mass outside his diocese.

27

Dear Fr Dunn,
I very much regret the Radharc treatment of planned giving on your programme last night, as expounded by the committeeman, without any answer.
I am,
Yours sincerely.

The programme in question concerned the building of a church in Dundalk where a member of the building committee voiced his objections to planned giving:

"These professional fundraisers may be able to bring in the money much faster, but I wonder at the end will they have preserved the goodwill of the parish and will they have prevented divisions within the parish arising out of this, if you like, blitzkrieg for funds."

During John Charles' reign, one of his biggest headaches was getting the clergy to accept planned giving. He engaged a professional group called Wells to help the parishes raise money for the new churches he wished to build in an expanding diocese. Parish priests who were reluctant to adopt the new system had to be sent a stiff reminder — "Get Wells cards", as they were christened by the jokers at the time. So the committeeman's criticism touched a sensitive spot.

Nobody would have believed it at the time, and some may not believe it still, but that letter on planned giving is the only recorded comment by John Charles on a Radharc programme. Proof I feel of a successful relationship!

I think I achieved this relationship by a careful analysis of the character of John Charles himself, and the characteristics of a bishop of the period, particularly a bishop who had exercised power for a considerable time. After a little experience, I set out some guidelines for myself to apply to all dealings with John Charles:

1. Accept his quasi omniscience
John Charles was a former schoolteacher. He had lived in France and was familiar with the classics. He had a retentive memory and was an excellent shot. He was informed about a lot of things, and for the rest, better not contradict him.

I remember one day sitting on the edge of the seat, desperately trying to get a decision out of him to release somebody to work with me, when suddenly he said, apropos of nothing, "which eye do you see best with Father?" I looked at him with one eye, and then with the other, perhaps a little over ostentatiously and confessed that I seemed to see equally well with both eyes. "Wrong Father," he said. And the index finger came up in a particularly characteristic fashion. He rose from the desk and walked around the room delivering a lecture on why one eye was always weaker than the other, while I tried to listen politely with one half of the brain and plan my next move with the other.

This little failing could of course work in one's favour. I knew he couldn't know very much about television so I tried to plant ideas in his head at an early stage in the hope, as sometimes happened, that they might come back later as his own.

Talking of omniscience, one of his more amusing letters related to our first trip to Africa. This meant a group of priests leaving the diocese for about five weeks, and quite apart from the Monaco affair, it was very reasonable to ask permission.

I explained how the Society for the Propagation of the Faith appeared willing to help pay our fares, and continued:

"Apart from the thrill of seeing real lions and tigers, I suggest the following reasons in favour of the trip: RTÉ have themselves begun to do some kinds of programmes that we have been doing in the past. However this kind of trip is something they will hardly be able to do and will help therefore to continue to make our contribution unique." And so on. (It's always nice to have three reasons).

My letter was dated 2nd of April, 1965.
The reply came almost immediately:

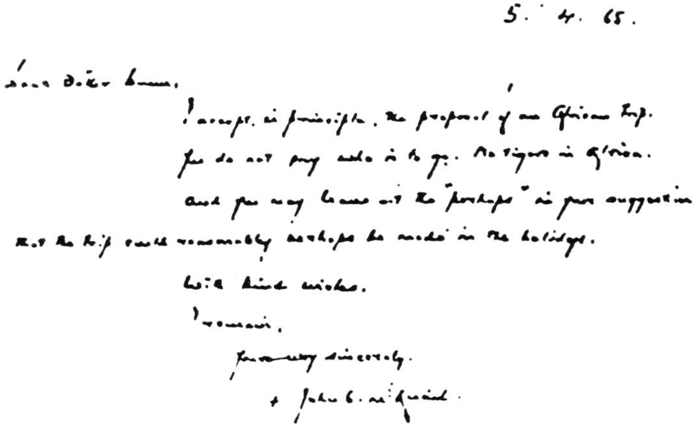
5. 4. 65.

Dear Father Dunn,

I accept in principle the proposal of an African trip.
You do not say who is to go. No tigers in Africa.
And you may leave out the "perhaps" in your suggestion
that the trip could reasonably perhaps be made in the holidays.

With kind wishes,
I remain,
Yours very sincerely,
+ John C. McQuaid.

Dear Fr Dunn,
I accept, in principle, the proposal of an African trip. You do not say who is to go. No tigers in Africa. And you may leave out the 'perhaps' in your suggestion that the trip could reasonably perhaps be made in the holidays.
With kind wishes.
I remain,
Yours very sincerely,
✠ John C McQuaid.

2. *Never ask for a decision which you haven't made yourself beforehand*
I used to spend long hours drafting and redrafting memos for John Charles — memos which could only reach the conclusion that I desired. John Charles had a retentive mind and he was a worker, so one could be assured, whatever else, that he would read what one sent to him and probably remember it for longer than one could remember it oneself.

The tricky situation arose when John Charles himself made some decision or even a suggestion which somehow had to be reversed without loss of face. In one memo outlining the difficulties in producing programmes when everyone with the interest and ability to contribute to Radharc was busy about other things, I also mentioned the problem of where to work, now that I was out of the University chaplaincy and living in digs.

I threw out some options without however being clear myself what I wanted. I got a letter back quickly:

My dear Father Dunn,
I wonder if Clonliffe could accommodate you for the moment? Would you mind calling on the President?
With kind wishes,
I remain,
Yours very sincerely.

That was the last place we wanted to be for several reasons, not the least of which was the symbolic one that apparently, if not actually, it would limit our independence.

Fortunately the President of Clonliffe, for his own reasons, was not happy about it either. So the task was to say that, while the suggestion was an excellent one, it was unfortunately impractical at present, for the following very cogent reasons . . .

I can still remember that I sweated for three days over the reply, drafting and redrafting, and eventually when it was written, the envelope addressed, sealed and stamped, I stood for several minutes at the letter box undecided whether to post it or have another go.

3. Prepare one's chat before any meeting

In my opinion, many people failed to strike up a relationship with John Charles because they were afraid to talk to him. He wasn't good at small talk himself. Neither was I, for that matter, but I used to prepare some chat beforehand and try to generate an atmosphere of warmth. Pull his leg gently sometimes or give him a little interesting information which he mightn't have heard elsewhere. Once he sensed one had warm feelings towards him — and I think I genuinely had — then he blossomed out and that charm appeared which some of his friends obviously experienced all the time, and which some of his priests never knew even existed.

4. Keep him informed of (nearly) everything

There were obvious dangers in this but much less than might first appear. He was most supportive of those he trusted and least likely to interfere with them. On the other hand, if he felt anyone was taking initiatives without his knowledge or permission then the fur could fly.

He was a master of the karate chop in written form. One of his secretaries told me once that they dreaded a morning when some visitor failed to turn up. John Charles would seize the opportunity to toss off letters at a rate of about one a minute in his unique spidery hand, all of which the secretaries had to photocopy and file.

And perhaps because he tossed out comments so fast, he couldn't have fully considered the shock effect that some of them would have on the recipients. There are, I am sure, thousands of these letters still around and they are one reason why poor John Charles may never be canonised.

The following are some mild examples:

I wrote to him about World Communications day which I was promoting in another capacity. Hinted that he might accept the national literature (which I had had a hand in preparing) but if he was writing his own letter, he might like to use some selected quotations from the Vatican II decree which I appended. He wrote back.

31

21.4.70

Dear Fr Dunn,
I thank you for your letter enclosing excerpts from the Council Decree. It is my intention to write my own letter to this diocese.
I remain,
Yours sincerely.

And then:

1.5.70

Dear Fr Dunn,
I have issued my own letter and Prayer of the Faithful for my diocese on Communications Sunday. U Thant* could have written your Prayer of the Faithful; no imprimatur.
I remain,
Yours sincerely.

Two further examples:

I had written to inform him that Father Mario Borelli, well-known at the time from the Morris West book *Children of the Sun*, had asked us to make a film in Naples to promote his work in England, where he had many supporters.

John Charles wrote back:

3.4.65

My dear Father,
Interesting! Borelli has to come to Dublin to have his work filmed. Accept his offer. Being Italian, he will draw the profits. I see he has lunched at the Nunciature and addressed social workers in my city.
Yours very sincerely.

And later that year, in November 1965 when I asked permission to attend the closing of the Vatican Council:

I am quite willing that you come to Rome for a brief period to meet missionary bishops — and journalists. The facile ignorance of some of the latter will enable you to understand the Council if not the Catholic Church.
With kind wishes.

*Buddhist Secretary General of UN.

32

One of my favourite stories about John Charles, which I also know to be true, concerns one of these letter writing episodes. Something went wrong with his pen and he threw it down in disgust. "Why can't I ever find a pen that works?" he complained. "They might work better if Your Grace didn't dip them so often in vitriol," the secretary replied. I don't know whether John Charles laughed, but the secretary was promoted to a curacy not too long afterwards.

Undoubtedly many people were hurt by his sarcasm, though I often felt that much of this sarcasm was meant to be humorous rather than hurtful. In practice anyway, I found the correct thing to do was to take it as such, laugh at it, and proceed as if no hurt was intended.

I wrote on 16 November 1969 asking for an appointment to see him. I mentioned that I was not free on Monday afternoon 17th, and would be tied up with meetings all day Wednesday 19th. But apart from that I would be free anytime. I had a reply the following day:

Dear Fr Dunn,
If your duties allow you to call on me, I shall be free to see you at 10.30 am on Thursday 20th inst. I appreciate the courtesy of being told in advance the exact points that you wish to mention.
I am,
Yours sincerely.

On his 25th anniversary as bishop he told the assembled Dublin clergy that he hoped to serve us to the end — meaning death. The end came rather sooner than he expected. The other bishops were a bit fed up with his "go it alone" policies and when he tendered his resignation at 75, as he had to do, it was accepted.

As well as tough letters, John Charles also wrote letters which were kind and supportive. He gave us money for equipment (which we paid back to the diocese later in the seventies) and he took a fatherly interest in their purchase:

15.4.67

My dear Father,
I am interested in the TV camera, French I think, that you described — having suffered so much from photographers. What is it exactly? What is its cost? What its usefulness? Must one expect

33

to hear that it too has been superceded by something still more wonderful?
With grateful regards.
I remain,
Yours very sincerely.

I was a little slow in replying.

25.4.67

My dear Father,
I am grateful for details of the Eclair camera. Rumination describes your speed of answer. I shall give you this Eclair for your better work.
You may order it at once.
With grateful regards.
I remain.

I wrote back:

My Lord Archbishop,
Your Grace's last letter left me not only ruminating but speechless. What do I say? I am looking out the window and failing to think up some suitable expression of thanks. But they all sound terribly trite. So I have to fall back on a simple thank you. Penny coloured, tuppence plain.
I remain.

His reply is dated the following day:

My dear Father,
I am grateful that the ten minutes looking through the window produced such swift results. Byron said "the grateful heart, by owing, owes not". Get the machine that you find best for your work.
With grateful regards.

When John Charles retired I wrote him a letter to wish him well.

He wrote back:

20.2.72

My dear Father,
I am slow in answering. You will pardon me. For your kindly

34

message of gratitude and good wishes I am indeed grateful. I hope you will have even greater opportunities of using your talents in the cause of the old faith. I will ask our Blessed Lady to secure for you that grace. And you will pray for me.
With my grateful regards.

In fact I never met him again and it's something I still feel badly about. He moved quite suddenly from a position of great power and activity to one where he was powerless, unemployed, and semi ostracised. Rightly or wrongly some seemed to suggest that to call at Killiney, where John Charles lived, might be taken as a symbol of opposition to the new regime. So I decided to wait a little.

As Archbishop, John Charles appeared to have a very strong constitution. I never remember him being ill. So there didn't seem any hurry. But he was dead in little over a year.

John Charles provided the initial training which made a project like Radharc possible. When needed, he supported it with money. When needed, he permitted priests to work for it. With the one or two exceptions mentioned, he never interfered.

His successor on the other hand reduced the available manpower and despite repeated requests never released any new blood to learn the business and assure continuity. But that's another story.

*We **are** in Africa aren't we?*

7

The first efforts

The original memo set out an ideal situation where a group would meet each morning for six to eight weeks to plan programmes and arrange their execution.

Needless to say it never happened that way. Apart from a trip to Donegal, most of the work was done in bits and pieces around Dublin on afternoons off.

Most items were about 8-10 minutes in length and the general aim was to have three or four in each programme.

Some items were blatant imitations of the BBC *Tonight* programme style, which meant that they had to have a funny ending — as newsreaders like to have nowadays at the end of the news bulletin.

So when we reported on the Glenties, Co Donegal, parish effort in the Tidy Towns Competition, Peter Lemass concluded his spiel, lit a cigarette and threw away the cigarette package. Immediately a carefully briefed young nipper shot into picture, grabbed the offending piece of litter and put it in the trash basket.

The stories which eventually aroused most comment were the longest and the shortest — one on the Gloucester Street Sodality, which lasted seventeen minutes, and two which involved little girls telling stories — one on the calling of the twelve apostles and the other on the apparitions at Lourdes:

> Once upon a time there was this place called Lourdes that's called after our chapel. And there was this family living in it, and one of the little girls' names was Bernadette, and she had asthma, like my cousint, and she do be coughin' all night. And this day

Our Lady and God were looking down from Heaven to pick somebody to disappear to eighteen times at the grohho in Lourdes. And there were hundreds and hundreds of kids. And so she picked Bernadette out of every one of them, and she disappeared to her eighteen times at the grohho of Lourdes. And she told her loads of messages . . .

There was a third story in the same genre about the devil which we never used. While it was very very funny, we felt that the child must have got the ideas from a teacher whose methods we couldn't approve of. I meant to keep it, but, alas! some time, somebody must have thrown it out.

The Sodality was a story about a group of dockers in Gloucester St who decided to drum up more members for the men's sodality by fair means or foul. Some of the characters had a Sean O'Casey ring about their speech which gave the story a particular quality.

Boxer Dowdall was one such character. We decided to interview him in the pub, because that's where one normally met him. For quietness sake it was done during the holy hour, though some illegal pints were produced by the helpful barman. Everything was ready to roll when Boxer confided that he was worried about his dirty trousers.

"No problem at all," I said, "I'll be shooting you tight." ("Tight" in television terms is another way of saying "close-up".) I learnt afterwards that Boxer took it to have another meaning.

So You'd like to shoot me tight.

37

Equipment

In conducting the mid-summer experiment, the aim was to be able to do whatever is normally done in television, though not necessarily to the highest standard. The difficult part was to find some system whereby sound and picture could be recorded in step with each other. We chose the cheapest workable system.

Editing of mute film was done in a simple viewer. Interviews with synchronous sound were edited on a synchroniser, without viewer. This entailed checking the picture with a magnifying glass. For the first few years we never saw a Radharc programme properly until it was being transmitted.

The first experimental programmes were completed before the most exasperating problem emerged. The hundred or so shots in each film had been stuck together with what was called a "universal" cement. Well, it wasn't universal enough. I learnt too late that I should have used a special cement made only for this film.

This problem emerged when the programmes began to disintegrate on the projector after one or two showings. Every join had to be recut and remade and the sound track adjusted accordingly. It was a painful procedure.

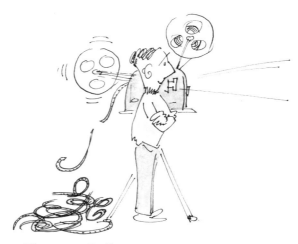

The name Radharc

I was responsible for deciding on the name Radharc, an Irish word meaning a view or a vision. The group had been through the Oxford dictionary looking for a title for the first programmes. The record says that I rejected all the suggestions. We were all agreed that a name must have some relevant meaning. At the same time, it had to be unusual if it were to stand out and be remembered. This was the problem. I remember being impressed by the title of an American programme *WHAAM* but couldn't think of any religious equivalent. It was Des Forristal's parish priest, Fr Michael Murphy, who suggested *Radharc*. Our first ever film had been in Irish. We had hoped within the context of a magazine programme to make more. But quite apart from the language and the meaning, I liked the sound Radharc and felt it might be different enough as a programme title to be remembered. It was certainly a welcome change from *Panorama, Viewpoint, Festival, Insight,* and many other similar names for programmes which keep turning up with slight variations on the British Channels.

The decision was probably a sound one so long as most of the country was limited to reception of RTÉ. But Ireland now has a relatively young population — fifty per cent under the age of twenty-five. Most of these have grown up accustomed to a multi-channel television. The word Radharc may suggest programmes in Irish which only a minority are willing to watch. So in the business of hunting viewers, I think the name may now be a bit of a liability. But I don't know what one can do about it, except try and give it the right kind of publicity. It is a hard thing to change your name!

The logo

The twelve apostles from the Moone cross provided us with a logo which I wouldn't ever want to change. Hopefully it symbolises something about the programme, this wide eyed, slightly amused and detached group looking out over the centuries on the changing scene; not only in Irish society, but in the wider community throughout the Christian world with which the Celtic Church was in close touch.

8

From experimental film to RTÉ programme

The programmes were edited by October and I wrote to John Charles asking him to come to see them.

He never came, which disappointed us.

We also tried to make it known to RTÉ that we had some samples of the kind of religious programmes we felt might be of interest to an Irish audience.

But nobody took any notice.

It seemed that after a lot of thought and effort, we would not be permitted to influence religious broadcasting. However, within a week or two of the service being due to open — and here I rely on memory — Pádraic Ó Raghallaigh, special assistant to the first Programme Controller Michael Barry, phoned up and said he'd come to see what we had to offer.

He arranged to come to the University Chaplaincy where I lived in two rooms at the top of a Georgian building. The front room, which was noisier, was used as an editing room. The back room was a bedsitter and recording studio rolled into one. I had knocked out a brick or two in the wall between the two rooms and fitted glass in the hole so that a film could be viewed in the bedroom without the obtrusive noise of the projector.

A few hours before he came, Mr Ó Raghallaigh phoned again to say he was bringing Michael Barry, the Programme Controller. This was more than we'd bargained for. So it was a very nervous priest who led two senior RTÉ executives up to the fourth floor. There were three programmes. I ran them one after the other, nearly one and a half hours. I didn't dare go back into the bedroom until the end — just twiddled my thumbs, hoped they'd stick it out, and the film wouldn't break into pieces.

Afterwards Michael Barry got up from his chair, strolled around the room asking a few questions and then sat on the bed.

From this undignified seat of office, the controller of programmes asked his assistant to arrange for the films to be shown on the new service as soon as possible.

Radharc on air

The first transmission was a deeply depressing experience. The film was transmitted five frames out of sync — lip movements and sound did not exactly correspond. The problem arose because of different technical standards between amateur and professional film projectors. It's a problem that could have been solved if anyone had realised it in time. But nobody did.

On the other hand, the reviews on succeeding days provided sweet music. The following is a selection:

"An experimental film *Radharc* . . . was the outstanding item on Telefís Éireann last night . . . this was a brilliant job of documentary reporting."

"There was, I truly believe, more human interest in this programme than anything Telefís Éireann has so far screened."

"This feature in the badly named *Radharc* was distilled television, the essence of the secret of the medium which hundreds of TV station directors are seeking."

"If you didn't see it you missed one of the best pieces of unrehearsed film reporting yet seen on Irish TV."

"The second *Radharc* film broadcast on Telefís Éireann last night was in ways even more praiseworthy than the first."

"One would not have been surprised to learn that the team responsible for this sequence was on loan from BBC TV's *Tonight*."

"*Radharc* improves on each outing."

"As an experiment these films may be voted outstandingly successful."

Nothing succeeds like success. With that kind of reviews, we could do no wrong.

An independent film unit comes to be

A lot of things about Radharc happened by accident. Some time after the programmes appeared on television, Michael Barry and

41

John Charles McQuaid happened to be attending the same public function. The two got talking together. Michael Barry spoke of *Radharc* with enthusiasm and apparently told John Charles that if he would permit us to make more programmes, he as Programme Controller would be glad to purchase them.

So the word came back to us through Canon Cathal McCarthy to the effect that if and when we decided what minimum equipment would be needed to work professionally on television, the Archbishop would be willing to pay for it.

9

Early films

One of the first films to be made with the new camera was a feature on *Christy Brown*. The late Christy was, of course, a spastic. We interviewed him all the same, which was considered a slightly daring thing to do at the time.

The story of *Kylemore Abbey* was conventional enough in religious programme terms, except that one of the present community in Kylemore told me recently that she felt she owed her vocation to it!

I remember during the film that members of the crew were disappearing for long periods and then re-appearing with guilty grins and mysterious smiles. The mystery was solved when during a lull a little nun pulled me aside and beckoned me to follow her to the basement, where it turned out she had a little cache of her own brew of parsnip wine. So it was my turn to return to the job with a smile on my face.

The Young Offenders, our first full length film, included interviews with prison officers and young detainees in St Patrick's institution. This required permissions which would be much more difficult to get today. The programme was rounded off by an interview with the then Justice Minister, Charles J Haughey. Mr Haughey agreed to be interviewed on condition that he saw the filmed report on St Patrick's first. I was then living on Mount Merrion Avenue, with a small editing machine in my bedsitter. Mrs Greene, the landlady, was very tolerant of the peculiar noises that came from my room most of the day and some of the night, but I think she got a bit of a shock one day when she found Mr Haughey knocking on her door.

Early on we tried a series of programmes on real life moral issues: they concerned such topics as *Poaching and Poachers, Honesty at the Fair* and *Smuggling and Smugglers.*

I am not sure that the programmes did much to improve morality in Ireland in any of these areas, but if they didn't, they at least provided some amusement. Each film had its quota of rogues and the script too had a light touch. I remember Des Forristal pointing out that there were two cattle marts in Keady, Co Armagh. The one on screen was for protestant cows. Catholic cows went to a different one down the street.

We knew Matt Talbot was filmed at odd moments over a long period. I haven't seen it recently, but there were nice pictures of Dublin in the early 1960s. Many of the places like Rutland Street, and T & C Martin's yard on the North Wall have of course disappeared. As indeed the people who knew Matt personally, and who talked about him in the film.

Fr Casey and the Land War was the first full length film on a historical subject. In summer 1963 there were still some old people in Abbeyfeale who had personal memories of the Land War and these we felt were worth preserving. The film won an international award which I didn't feel it quite deserved. But I've always been interested in history and have a bias towards historical subjects which programme controllers and others have tried at times to keep in check. The Land War was the first of many historical films, and I don't regret any of them.

Down and Out in Dublin was probably a bit ahead of the field in the social sphere. The technique, which we learnt quickly, was to set up cameras wherever the subject of the film tended to congregate and then sit around and chat for about half an hour or an hour. When the novelty of seeing cameras and microphones had worn off and people understood what we were at, they tended to forget their inhibitions and say what they thought.

Politics as a Career was an attempt to try something different.

In the end we decided to open the film with a political meeting addressed by James Tully on a Sunday morning outside a parish church. Shortly after the cameras started to roll, and Mr Tully was in full flight on the evil machinations of his political opponents, the Angelus bell struck. Without drawing a breath he made the sign of the cross and swung into "The Angel of the Lord declared Unto Mary". God be with the days!

"The Angel of The Lord Declared Unto Mary."

1963 saw a trip to England which was the first foray abroad. The Irish Church was running a chaplaincy scheme for emigrants working in hostels, factories, building sites, etc. Among others we interviewed Cardinal Heenan, Archbishop of Westminster — himself a confident and experienced television performer. When we had fitted the small lapel mike on his soutane he told us that it would be better moved to another position! Which annoyed Peter Lemass at the time, and left the rest of us amused.

During this period the favourable reviews continued. One of the ones that tickled me at the time came from *The Sunday Press*, 22.12.1963. The context was an interview with the Minister responsible for broadcasting, Michael Hilliard. "The Minister enjoys going to country fairs, or taking a look at his cattle", we were told. "His favourite TV programme is Radharc . . . they have such wonderful interviewers".

By 1965 we had achieved a measure of confidence and some method and facility in the making of film. The time seemed ripe to stretch our wings a little and see the world.

10

Africa

Our first big trip abroad was to Africa. There were several other visits in later years, but the memories of the first one have lasted the longest.

We prepared for about six months, reading everything from Elspeth Huxley to technical data on how to keep lenses and film from going mouldy in tropical countries.

Because we were going on the missions, however temporarily, we were entitled to go by Raptim, a Dutch charitable agency which subsidises missionary travel: This meant going Dublin/ Amsterdam/ Nairobi return for £66, a very good price even then.

The plane to Amsterdam was an ordinary scheduled flight. But thereafter the flight was a special one — a Boeing 707 full of missionaries, pampered all the way to Nairobi. Drinks were on the house, everyone received a range of gifts, including slippers and chocolate and cigars — none of your cheroots, but full-sized Schimmelpennick coronas. It was a noisy boisterous crowd of nuns and clerics that spilled out on the tarmac in Nairobi.

We were in late at night and my memories of Africa begin the next morning with that unpleasant sweaty feeling that comes with saying Mass in the tropics in full Roman vestments. After Mass, out into a garden alive with tropical birds, like the aviary in the Zoo, except this was the real thing.

There were five of us on the trip, and a Kiltegan priest who came with us most of the time as a guide. Plus a lot of heavy equipment. So we were advised to buy two cars and sell them again when we were leaving. The missionaries knew someone who would give us a good deal. We used these cars, a Volkswagen and a Hillman, around Nairobi and up as far as Kitale, and even Ortum. But once it came to desert areas or mountains, we had to fall back on the landrovers or small aeroplanes.

The road accident rate is very high in East Africa; while we were fortunate enough not to have any ourselves, we passed by several which put the fear of God into us. The worst was where two lorries crammed with Africans collided on a hill outside Nairobi: one overturned and dumped its human cargo down an embankment. Two ambulances, converted VW vans, arrived and the dead and injured were piled in one on top of the other like bodies going to the gas oven.

There were plenty of motoring stories going around among the missionaries. How one Irishman met a rhinoceros on the road to Mombasa who didn't like his red Volkswagen, and tried to turn

Now put it down! Good girl.

it over with his horn shoved under the front bumper (and very nearly succeeded). Or the story of Medical Missionaries of Mary who were caught by a flash flood. Most of the time the desert rivers are dry, and one gets used to crossing large river beds with complete nonchalance. But every now and again it rains in Uganda or somewhere and the water rushes down like a miniature tidal wave, sweeping all before it. The Irish sisters were caught one day in their Volkswagen by one of these flash floods and before they knew where they were, they and their VW were sailing toward Ethiopia at breakneck speed. Fortunately for them the car stuck temporarily in some bushy trees about half a mile downstream so they could clamber out and climb up into the branches. Two hours later the floods subsided and the nuns descended. But the VW had disappeared never to be found again.

Bush flying

I'm less afraid of commercial flying than travelling in a motor car. But small plane flying in third world countries is statistically risky. One does it when it's part of the job and leaves the rest in the hands of God.

In Africa we used a missionary flying service operated by an American teaching brother in Nairobi who enjoyed flying in his spare time. Brother Mike was a very clever pilot, though some said he took too many chances. He'd had a few minor accidents and had recently smashed a propeller when antelope ran across the runway while he was coming in to land. His great problem was how to purchase a new propeller and get the other damage repaired without letting the authorities know that there had been an accident. Mike's eyesight wasn't the best, and his spectacles looked like the bottom of beer bottles: he feared that if he came to the notice of the authorities his licence might be revoked.

I had two memorable flights with him. In the first instance we set out to take some aerial pictures of the mission at Ortum, which was situated in a valley surrounded by lightly wooded hills. Mike did several tight low turns in the valley while I hung out the window in the slipstream taking the pictures. It wasn't the nearby treetops passing in circular motion above and below that filled me with fright so much as the sound of the hooters in the wings put there to warn of an impending stall — they wailed incessantly. Mike was flying at the edge of flying. I knew enough about aeroplanes to know that we didn't have enough height to recover should a sudden downdraft put him over the edge.

48

The filming completed we proceeded down the valley. For the first time I noticed that the man sitting in the rear seat looked decidedly ashen. George was also an experienced US pilot, who had arrived in Africa the week before to help with the missionary flying, and had come on this trip to study the airstrips and routes. He turned to me and whispered nervously, "If I was Mike I'd be doing this 2,000 feet higher."

By this time we were nearing the end of the valley, the hills on each side towered above us and we appeared to be flying straight into a rock wall. However, Mike knew his terrain; within spitting distance of the cliff, he banked sharply right and shot through a narrow defile and out over the Turkana desert.

On another occasion Mike was to bring Peter Lemass and myself from Kitale to the Medical Missionaries of Mary Hospital in Lorugumu, Northern Kenya, a distance of about 150 miles.

We expected him to arrive about 3 pm, but he didn't appear until several hours later. About half an hour from sunset he announced he was ready to leave.

"It's too late Mike," I said, "Let's leave it till tomorrow."

"Either we go now, or we don't go at all," said Mike, "I've got to be in Nairobi tomorrow."

Now Lorugumu was an eight to ten hour journey by landrover, down a steep escarpment and across dried-up river beds and deserts, so there wasn't a lot of choice. We took off into the setting sun. Soon afterwards dusk set in and dusk doesn't last long in the tropics. Mike indicated some tall mountains on the port side and informed us that they were the only things higher than we were and therefore the only things we needed to avoid. Having passed them we would set a course by compass for Lorugumu, about four or five thousand feet nearer sea level than our starting point. So making the required adjustment for wind speed and direction, and adopting a gentle gliding descent, we should see somebody waving a torch in one hour and four minutes time.

By this time we were flying in complete blackness, blackness that I had never experienced before. There were no towns, no roads, no sign of human life except the very occasional pinpoint of red light from the camp fire of some wandering Turkana. I sat there suspended in darkness, surrounded by the dull roar of the engine, and said to myself, "you've been in some crazy situations, but this is one of the craziest."

When the time came for the torchlight to appear, it didn't. Minutes ticked by with at least two of the three of us rapidly approaching a state of panic. Then five minutes after the ETA Peter was the first to see a flash of light. Mike immediately threw the plane into a turn. Another stronger light appeared which we learnt later were Volkswagen van lights marking the end of the runway. I tried hard to make out what was happening but before I could get any bearings the undercarriage slapped on to the desert floor and we pulled up quickly in a cloud of dust.

Later that evening when Mike was relaxed with a good meal inside and a glass of beer in his hand, I asked him what he would have done if we hadn't found the torch. He had enough fuel, he said, to get back to Nairobi, the only place in Kenya where one can safely land at night. I was personally happy to feel we hadn't had to take that option — whatever about the hills, the *road* from Nairobi to Kitali reaches 10,000 feet.

"And what if we'd had a technical problem and had to come down before Lorugumu?" In that case he would have adopted a gentle glide path, keeping flying speed to a minimum. The chances of walking away from the plane after a blind landing in the desert, he estimated, were better than nine out of ten.

Next morning, we noted that the landing strip at Lorugumu had one other navigational aid which might have been activated if we had missed the torch. A long line of brushwood stretched on either side of the runway, which was simply a bit of desert cleared of big stones and bushes. The brushwood was tinder dry and only needed a match to explode into flames and light up the countryside for miles around.

Turkana

Turkana is both a place and a people. The place is bordered by the Sudan on the north, Uganda on the west and Lake Rudolf on the east.

When we first went there in 1965 many Turkana were dying of starvation. People were crowding around the mission station in emaciated condition, children with pot bellies, adults with dried up breasts and bones sticking out through skin. It reminded me of engravings I had seen of the Irish famine.

Food for the famine victims was low, even at the mission, and everybody was waiting impatiently for the lorry of maize to arrive. It came that evening. The people were forced back as the sacks were taken off the lorry and put in the store. It was too late that day to set up the procedure of weighing and distribution. It would have to be done in the morning.

And so the doors of the store were locked and the lorry drove away. But the people still pushed and stumbled forward and fought with each other to rescue a few grains of yellow maize that had spilled on the ground. I filmed a tall Turkana man, skin and bone, trying to bite into one of the iron-hard yellow grains. And hated myself for doing so.

The sad thing about this famine, and all the others that afflicted the Turkana down the ages, was that it was totally unnecessary. The Turkana tend their flocks of goats and camels and cattle, and live on a diet of blood, milk and cheese. The blood is drawn from the cattle by cutting a vein in the neck and gathering it in a bowl. The cheese is made by curdling the milk with cows' urine. Sometimes they eat meat and grain. But they preferred their cattle live rather than dead, and grain had to be purchased as no grain grew in the desert.

When the rains failed, as they periodically did, and there was nothing for the cattle to eat, the cattle died; and then there was nothing for the people to eat, so the people died; which was doubly sad because the Turkana lived beside one of the largest lakes in the world which was full of high protein fish.

In 1965 the missionaries had only just begun to teach the Turkana how to catch fish. The fishing stories were unbelievable. One could throw a fishing line in from the shore and catch 300lbs of fish within an hour. With heavy tackle one could trawl from a boat and catch Nile perch six feet long.

We went out one day to film the Turkana fishing. Lake Rudolf is famous for its crocodiles as well as its big fish; we had hopes of going on to an island where they gathered in large numbers.

Now the fishing grounds were some distance from the shore so we left very early, to escape the hot sun. The boats were built locally for use with oars, but we had a powerful engine. Maybe half an hour or three quarters from the shore, there was a loud cracking noise and the chap in charge quickly cut down the engine — it was too powerful for the boat, and had pushed itself through the transom! There was a second boat with us, but it was too small to take both parties. So it had to go back and get help.

Luckily it was a calm day — Lake Turkana can be very violent. We just sat there with little or no protection from the sun and waited for several hours. We all got burned, but Billy Fitzgerald suffered most. His feet swelled up like balloons and he was out of commission for several days. And we never got to the island of crocodiles.

The Turkana are a Nilo-hamitic people related to the better known Masai, who are also cattlemen and nomads. They are thought to have come down the Nile valley from the north — hence the name Nilo-hamitic.

Women wore a few skins around the middle, and men often but not always had a piece of material which they carried over the shoulder, to protect their body from sun and their face from flying dust. The women had circular ornaments in bright coloured beads around the neck or wrists. The men confined ornamentation to a mudcap, worn at the top and back of the head. This was often painted with bright colours and ornamented with beads, pieces of coloured glass, feathers etc, or even, as I saw in one instance, beer bottle tops. Since the cap could be damaged or cracked by contact with the ground, the men had to carry a small stool to prop up their heads while they slept. It looked a most uncomfortable way to sleep but clearly some such device was necessary. The other problem about mudcaps is that lice find the space between the cap and the scalp a very congenial sheltered place to live and breed in. It was quite a common sight to see men trying to get at the lice using pointed sticks pushed up between the mudcap and scalp.

The other item without which no well-dressed Turkana man would appear was a spear. The spear was elegant and fine — more like a narrow lance with a large arrowhead at one end, and a pointed goad at the other. The goad was used to prod the cattle, the shaft was used as a kind of prop to lean on in social conversation, and the whole spear was used like a lance to kill small animals or birds for food. No doubt they could also be used to kill people. Cattle raiding was a traditional pastime among the Turkana, and there were plenty of stories told of brushes with the Karamoja on the West, the Suk down South, and various other tribes in the Southern Sudan. I remember once driving on a desert road at night and catching two or three Turkana men in the car headlights, armed as they always were with two or three spears, and thinking as we covered them with dust, how easy it would have been for them to stop us with the point of a spear in the tyre. And if I were a Turkana, how tempting it might have been!

Billy Fitzgerald had several Turkana spears thrown at him on another occasion. The Medical Missionaries ran a small aeroplane to fly the Sister Doctor around the mission stations in the desert. Billy was commissioned to go up with Sister Pilot and try some aerial photography of desert scenes. Seeing some Turkana driving a herd of goats, they swooped low to get a better picture. It didn't work because the noise of the low flying plane scattered the goats, to the understandable annoyance of the Turkana, who threw their spears in anger at the aeroplane!

We were fascinated by the Turkana but I can't claim that we ever communicated with the adults — language difficulties apart, the cultural differences were too great. But the children who swarmed around the mission were different. They were full of energy and fun, and hadn't yet acquired the inhibitions that adults collect in every culture.

The other things that added piquancy to life in Turkana were the fauna and the insects. Leopards were not uncommon at the time, and with the drought and consequent scarcity of food, they had to become bolder to survive.

The medical Missionaries had had a favourite alsatian, and shortly before we arrived the poor animal had been carried off by a leopard or maybe a puma. We heard all the details of this recent sad bereavement shortly after our arrival. The nuns were naturally distraught and to help relieve their grief, some friends had presented them with a cat.

Our beds were on the verandah and we slept covered only by a sheet. On the second night Des Forristal woke everybody with a scream. The new domestic cat had just made a four-paw landing on his stomach. The precise species of cat family are a little difficult to distinguish in the space between sleep and a sudden awakening by claws and paws.

Billy Fitzgerald also had an interesting night-time experience. Waking up in the early hours of the morning, he found a tall naked tribesman with spear standing at the end of the bed — again it was on an open verandah. He sat up with a jolt and the man fled. He seemed to have a peculiar flapping hat on his head as he disappeared into the night. The next morning when Billy went to dress, his underpants were missing.

But to return to the fauna and creepy crawly things. Scorpions were common; one could easily find specimens to study under any stone. They could kill a child but adults usually survived, though with considerable pain. One of the nurses got a sting on one of our visits, but was ok after three days. Hunting spiders, large hairy fellows were also the subject of many lurid stories. We killed two of them one night and left their bodies in the corner. Next morning there was nothing left except hairs and hard bits. The ants had eaten the rest.

Snakes were common. There was a large hill about half a mile from the mission station at Lorugumu which was reported to be full of them. A team from some university had picked up two hundred specimens for study on one week-end.

The fact that they were plentiful didn't mean that one saw them often however. They are largely nocturnal animals and like to avoid human beings if they can possibly help it. But to walk in darkness in areas like Turkana without a torch was to play a kind of Russian roulette. I remember asking about a European who had built a house on the shores of Lake Turkana, only to be told that he had died six months before our visit. He went out for a walk one morning and stepped on a snake. The poison killed him in twenty minutes.

Snakes that were foolish enough to enter the mission compound were dispatched unceremoniously by the chaplain with the whack of a hurling stick. Or so we were told anyway.

Knit one, drop one!

The end of an era

One of the things that made the 1965 trip memorable is the fact that we were witnessing the beginning of the sudden transition of people like the Pokot and Turkana from a stone age to a high technological culture.

One day we recorded a group of Pokot women singing and then played it back. They had never seen or heard or imagined a tape recorder before.

The elders and people of an area of Pokot decided they would like to hear something more about western medicine. So they gathered at a crossroads in the bush on a predetermined day and we went out in the landrover with Leo Staples, a Kiltegan missionary, to meet them. The talking went on all day, and for us who had to sit and wait it was incredibly boring. But this was the tribal way of conducting formal discussion, and no white man's impatience would change it. After the formal proceedings there was a small feast and a big dance. Not the bogus sanitised African folk dance that one might see nowadays in a hotel in Nairobi or Mombasa, but something smelly, dusty, gutsy — the real thing.

Less than five years later, when I was next in Africa, I noticed a big change. Driving in East Pokot, we stopped the landrover to talk to a young boy looking after grazing cattle. He had a few brown rags about his middle, a stick to goad the cattle and a small transistor. He told us that the first man had landed that day on the moon.

Jomo Kenyatta

In 1965 Jomo Kenyatta, President of Kenya, was already four years in office. From the hated Mau Mau leader he had become the darling of the international press. Some of the Irish Holy Ghost Fathers had helped Jomo when he was on the run and he didn't forget it of them when he came into his kingdom. So when we wanted to film the President there was no problem.

Jomo himself was well aware of the importance of television in helping to weld the different tribes in Kenya together into one nation under his presidency. He had his own personal television crew which followed him everywhere. The main items on the Kenyan television news every evening were the doings of the President.

We had tea with Jomo one afternoon in a summer house in the grounds of the presidential palace at Gatundu.

I think the occasion was the President's birthday; anyway, some girls from the local convent school run by Irish nuns came up to entertain him. He sat with a friend of his, Fr Gannon, and watched with moderate interest as the girls performed some Kikuyu dances wearing traditional dress. This act was followed by a second troop of young Kikuyu ladies dressed in green kilts who gave an exhibition of Irish dancing. It was different from any Irish dancing I had ever seen — not so much in the variations of hallowed steps as in the freedom of movement and the general air of gaiety and grace, so characteristic of the African.

Watching Jomo was just as interesting as watching the dancing. The air of polite boredom had vanished. He slapped his knee and laughed heartily and made wisecracks all around him.

I remember thinking at the time that it was the kind of thing that we would be almost afraid to mention at home. It would sure as sure have been condemned as chauvinism of the worst kind — turning black babies into Irish schoolchildren. Looking back on it nowadays however, one might take a more relaxed view.

If there were African nuns running a school in Ireland, everybody would be delighted if they taught the children some Kikuyu dancing in addition to whatever our local culture has to offer.

One thing struck me very forcibly in the new state of Kenya — and the process was one in which the Irish played an important part. All the ministers in the first government of Kenya, from Jomo Kenyatta downwards, were trained in mission schools. The change in society came very rapidly. Kenyatta had never met a white man, let alone a teacher before he was fourteen years old.

We attended a function, the laying of the foundation of Mohoho High School to be run by Irish sisters near Gatundu, in the President's constituency. So the President came to the ceremony. There was a long tent-like awning where the important people sat. Jomo arrived to presidential fanfare and sat in the middle. On his left hand, his very much younger wife, Mama Ingena. Beside her, her brother, a Catholic priest of the diocese of Nairobi. At Jomo's right hand, Chief Mohoho, his father-in-law, who arrived after him. The Chief was accompanied by his thirteen wives and some small children. Jomo stood up in respect when his father-in-law arrived — the wisdom of age is very much respected in the African tradition. The first African President of Kenya, flanked by his father-in-law with thirteen wives on one side, and his wife and brother-in-law, a celibate Catholic priest on the other. This scene said something about the changes that had occurred in Africa in one lifetime.

There were several boring speeches which we didn't pay much attention to and then a white robed priest — a Holy Ghost Father with a reputation for sanctity — was called to pray for rain. The area around Gatundu hadn't had a drop of rain for over six months and there was a serious drought. Well, the priest had barely sat down before the clouds began to roll up. Suddenly the whole ceremony speeded up and people began to move for the exits. The sky got dark and the exodus became a stampede. It was only later on that we learned why.

The foundation stone for the hospital was being laid in a field and there was about half a mile of murrum road to be traversed before one reached the tar. Now murrum has a surface of hard earth with about two inches of red dust on top. Surface water takes some time to penetrate so after a shower of rain there remains the hard layer underneath, an inch or two of dust, and a layer of creamy mud on top. Even four wheel drive isn't a lot of use on such a surface. By the time we'd got the message, packed up our equipment and got moving, we were fairly far down the queue.

Just outside the car park there was a hollow with a hill up the other side. The cars had to take it one at a time, waiting in turn. It required considerable judgement to gauge the downhill speed so there would be just enough to get up the other side but not so much as to lose control on the way down. Some went down too fast, and sideswept the bank at the bottom which didn't do their bodywork much good. Others like a group of Irish Sisters were too slow on the way down and got stuck in the rise. Five nuns in white habits, beautifully laundered for the big occasion, had to get out in the mud and push their car up and out of the way.

But nobody minded. The day had been a resounding missionary success. Those clouds that appeared when the priest prayed would probably do more for the Kikuyu church than 20,000 sermons.

Cutting strips off the film

The African trip in 1965 was a great success and earned us an UNDA award, which was the religious programmes equivalent of an international Oscar. But it nearly turned into a technical disaster. Although the trip provided some of the best and most memorable moments in my life, it also provided some of the worst.

We had gone to Africa with a lot of hoo-ha — pictures in the paper and press notices everywhere. And fully three weeks into a five-week trip, we hadn't got one usable piece of interview in the can.

The trouble first came to light in Ortum, which is a long way from Nairobi over rough roads and down a steep escarpment. The Auricon camera we used was a combined camera and tape recorder. The film had a magnetic coating along one edge and the sound was recorded in the camera on the side of the film. One of the disadvantages of this system is that one can't replay a sound track until the film is developed. Which means in practice, until after one goes home. Now in Ortum we began to get what are called drop-outs — in simple terms the sound drops in level and quality for varying periods, some short, some long. We had had a similar problem once before and it was put down at the time to a faulty playback amplifier which had no effect on the actual recording. Being an intermittent problem, we couldn't get it fixed because it wouldn't appear when the engineer was around.

So I decided to record a short interview for test purposes, take out the film, and with a guide and razor blade set into a table, trim a quarter-inch wide strip off the side of the film containing the magnetic stripe. This was then rewound on a spool and played through an ordinary tape recorder. The recording tests all seemed fine. I did these tests with the faster of our two film stocks because we weren't using it very much.

Since we had made all our transport arrangements, including flights; and since the nearest place we could make a proper check was several hundred miles away; and since the fault seemed to be in the playback amplifier as before, and not in the recording, I made the decision to go ahead.

We went to Turkana. It was a great story. But the intermittent drop outs became more frequent, and I became more worried. When we finished we flew back to Nairobi to develop some of the film and do a proper test on a film projector.

The fault *was* in the recording. So most if not all the interviews filmed so far must be considered useless, probably not worth developing. It was a bad moment.

We went to the Voice of Kenya, the National Radio and TV Station, put our case and they generously loaned us an Auricon sound amplifier. We did tests in Nairobi which seemed to show all was well, and arranged to fly back northwards.

As soon as we started filming in the warmer semi-desert areas, the problem returned. So it couldn't be the amplifier. What's left? The recording head! Billy Fitzgerald took a flight back to Nairobi and called the Voice of Kenya — this time to beg them for a sound head. Once again they were generous. Back to Turkana with the precious head — round trip 700 miles. Start to interview amused and puzzled medical missionaries for the *third* time. Same problem. My God! What's left?

Only the film. The magnetic stripe is lifting off and clogging up the soundhead! But all our film came from the same manufacturer — sixty cans, 400 ft each. It was late in the trip to start looking for more film. And would it be any different from what we had? Perhaps Auricon cameras and striped film don't work in the heat of the desert?

It was Peter Lemass who said, "Try the fast film."

Although made by the same manufacturer, fifteen of the cans were fast film, which we hadn't used much because there was plenty of light around and we hadn't been shooting many interiors.

Now in theory the stripe should have been identical on each type of film, but perhaps, please God perhaps, they had put in a bit more glue in the mixture the day the fast film was made.

So we set about interviewing Sister Pilot for the fourth time, using the fast film and a deep filter to try and cut down the bright desert light. There was no trouble. Then another interview — no trouble: than a talk to camera: OK! I cried in a corner with sheer relief.

So the problem was that one batch of our film — which unfortunately happened to be 75% of the total — had a faulty magnetic stripe which in certain conditions of heat and humidity clogged up the soundheads. But we didn't have enough fast film. Back to Nairobi to hunt up stock. We took all that was available and it was only just enough.

This was the first but by no means the last technical problem that arose in distant countries over the years. Murphy's law says that things work against man. It seems to apply more often than usual to film making.

Radharc in Africa
Five programmes were eventually produced under this title. Two of them concerned themes which we would pick up again in other countries. *New Voices* dealt with the struggles of a church which wants to be part of its own people, rather than a carbon copy of a European original. *The Problems* dealt with the concerns of the church in a very new situation. Independence was a watershed in the history of the Kenya mission, and in 1965 missionaries were trying to come to terms with it.

The other programmes dealt with different areas of mission in which Irish people were involved: *Kikuyu Country,* homeland for the dominant tribe in Kenya, *Forbidden Valley,* where the Suk tribe lived, and *Turkana.*

I remember looking at a print of *Turkana* on Christmas morning 1965 in a flat in my mother's house where I was then living and working, and saying to myself aloud, "You've made at least one interesting film." The Turkana — a tall good-looking people untouched by the twentieth century; famine in the land; young Irish nuns flying aeroplanes here and there to bring them succour. It was surefire material and we didn't need to be great artists to put together a good story.

Turkana won the UNDA international award at Monte Carlo, and was shown on BBC, CBS (Canada) and in the USA, Belgium, West Germany, Holland and New Zealand.

60

11

Tuppence worth from every penny

Radharc has always been a part-time activity for most of the people who contribute. It is important therefore to make maximum use of the time part-timers are willing or able to give. So Radharc trips tend to be full if not hectic. We don't have time to waste sitting around getting over jet lag. When we arrived in Sydney, Australia in 1978, straight from Ireland, we filmed an interview on the way from the airport!

Our rate of filming abroad is about one half hour of finished film every week. However, a trip last summer to the United States which included locations in Washington, Arizona, Los Angeles, San Francisco, and Seattle yielded the equivalent of seven half-hour programmes in less than five weeks.

Cutting corners? It depends on what you mean. I'm satisfied that the programmes were worthwhile and I am happy to put my name to them. Could they have been better if we spent twice as long in the States? Yes. And they could have been still better if we spent six months working on each of them, which is what a BBC producer might expect to spend. But the difference wouldn't be all that great; and we couldn't afford it; and I don't think Telefís Éireann *should* be able to afford it. We in Ireland are making television for a country with one-twentieth of the population, and therefore one-twentieth of the income that British TV has to make programmes. That's not a reason for making shoddy-cheap programmes. But it is a reason for not Rolls Roycing. It's a reason for not shooting fifteen times the amount you need in the hope of getting that outstanding shot which may turn the film into a work of art, but not make it say much more than it would have said anyway.

Or to put it in a nutshell, I think it is more important for RTÉ to make six interesting films that are worth showing to an Irish audience, rather than one interesting programme which may win some obscure award.

In 1966, the year after Africa, we went to the Far East. Des Forristal, being an organised kind of person kept a diary of the trip. The following is the record of a day in the life of Radharc in the Philippines, based on his diary and my recollection:

4.00 am	Explosion rocks the town of Kabankalan, Negros Occidental, Philippine Islands. Turn over on straw mattress and try to sleep again.
4.10 am	Another louder explosion.
4.20 am	Third explosion. Sleep out of the question. Anyway driver calling at 5.30.
4.45 am	Arrive at church for Mass. Someone explains the explosions are in honour of the approaching feast.
5.30 am	Toast and coffee. Check the equipment. Everyone half asleep and probably in bad humour. No one talks.
6.30 am	Should be at Salong to film parish mission, but driver failed to turn up. Much agitation.
7.00 am	On the road at last. VW minibus makes heavy weather of the rutted track winding between fields of tall sugar cane. We carry delicate

	equipment in our hands to cushion bumps. It's pouring rain.
7.45 am	Salong with charming wooden houses among tall palm trees looks highly photogenic. Rain stops. Spirits rise.
7.50 am	Spirits sink. Because of the delay the function is over. Consultation. Perhaps the people would like to hold the ceremony which we tried to film yesterday, but which was abandoned because of rain?
8.50 am	A couple of hundred villagers are lined up with flags and banners to welcome the two missioners to their village. Jeep will drive up and stop at a point marked with a white stone. After meeting the village elders, whole procession will lead off in the direction of the village plaza. The director shouts 'rolling' and the action commences.
9.10 am	Scene 1. Take 1. Action was ragged. The jeep stopped at the wrong place. And the sound was poor.
9.50 am	Scene 1. Third take OK. Proceed to plaza for work on ceremony. Half the chairs and benches are in shadow, half in sun. So they have to be rearranged. The shooting continues to 10.45 am.
11.00 am	Coffee, fried eggs and fresh pineapple offered by the lady with whom the missioners are staying.
11.15 am	We film missioners visiting houses. They visit one house four times for sake of the camera.
11.45 am	Walking interview through village. Wires all over the place. Everybody walking backwards through Philippino village in the mid-day sun.
12.30 pm	Pack equipment and move.
1.15 pm	Lunch in Kabankalan, with Fr Doohan and Fr Niall O'Brien. (*Later famous as one of the Negros Nine*)
2.00 pm	Rest for those who can afford it.
2.45 pm	Pack the gear, hit the road. Head for Sumag, 80 miles away for closing of Samaria — a kind of week-end retreat for sugar workers at which some spectacular conversions have taken place. Several men expected to confess publicly to murder.
4.30 pm	Sumag — a strip of beach, row of coconut palms,

63

and the Samaria house behind the high wall. Commence filming immediately. Interior and exterior shots, two interviews, and recording of Samaria songs.

6.00 pm   Sunset. End of filming. Lights are promised from Bacolod and we can do nothing until they arrive. If they arrive. Someone produces coca cola and hot dogs.

7.30 pm   Lights arrive. Also the crowds. Naked bulbs are being hung from wires between the trees. Just about enough light with fastest lens and film.

8.15 pm   Two cameras ready to roll. No rehearsal this time. Difficult to know what to do. We let the speeches pass. Then series of morality plays. Film a bit. But it's not really what we came for.

10.00 pm   The climax of the ceremony. One by one each of the seventy men come to the microphone and say in his own words what the Samaria has meant for him. Emotion charged atmosphere. Many break down and weep. For these men conversion has become a reality. With a bit of luck may have got some of the better ones on film.

11.00 pm   Spatter of rain and then the storm suddenly breaks. Hold on to the gear and protect it from the wet as the crowds scramble past. Into the car and repack out of the wet.

11.30 pm   Rain cleared. Extra sound effects need to be recorded.

12.00   On the road again.

12.30 am   The room in the hotel Majorca, Bacolod, contains five beds, just the right number.

1.00 am   Blissful sleep.

What's missing from any such account, and which is very difficult to communicate, is the uncertainty of it all. It's not very tiring to do something. It's much more tiring to have to make decisions as to what to do!

We didn't expect to be late for our first appointment, so we had to change plans. What we did in the first village depended entirely on the willingness of the villagers to put themselves out to a considerable extent, and the ability of the local priest to motivate them to do so.

Our visit to Sumag had not been scheduled. But when we heard about the Samaria at lunch, it seemed it could be an important addition to our film.

On the eighty mile journey, Niall O'Brien got cold feet, and felt that a European audience wouldn't understand the weeping and display of emotion. Perhaps we shouldn't film it. Perhaps it was exploiting the people. More arguments, more decisions.

The Samaria was a three-hour event. How does one choose the important bits? And how do you know when they are going to occur? Decisions, decisions, decisions.

Six programmes came out of this Asian trip. The events of that particular day appeared in a film about sugar workers in the Philippines called *The Restless Knives*. A Dutch television producer told me recently that he remembered it being shown in Holland, and that he considered it to be what he called "a seminal film" which had had a lot of influence on the direction of their work at the time.

12

Difficult and dangerous places

I was anxious that we should cover the story of the war in Nigeria and pressed the idea of a trip to Biafra at Radharc meetings. But I had another job full of problems at the time and couldn't go; Des Forristal, Peter Lemass, Peter Canning and Dermod McCarthy made up the team that eventually travelled. It was only when they had gone that the danger element in the trip struck home to me. I woke one day in a cold sweat having dreamed they were in a plane crash. It turned out not to be true — but not to be too far from the truth either.

They journeyed from Copenhagen to Sao Tome, an island off the coast of Nigeria, in a DC 6 which was carrying dried fish for the starving Biafrans. The flights were in small hops, Rome, Casablanca, and so on to Sao Tome.

When the team reached Sao Tome there was discussion whether to go straight in to Biafra or stay for a day and have a rest. A Holy Ghost priest ended the argument. "The best pilot," he said, "is McCombey. He's going in an hour or two — why not go with him?"

The journey was dangerous, particularly towards the end. The Federals had powerful jets. They didn't wish to run the risk of bad publicity by shooting down a "mercy plane". The trick was to bomb the roadway between Port Harcourt and Ihiala (which was the main and only runway) just before the Biafran plane hit the tarmac. This way the plane crashed on the ground, not in the air.

The landing had to be made in the dark and the lights flashed on and off for a few seconds near touchdown. The flight was completed without incident — Radharc had landed safely in Biafra. But the next night poor McCombey's plane hit a tree and cut a path a half mile long through the jungle. There were no survivors.

Night flight to Uli created a bit of a stir at the time. David Dimbleby in long mohair coat came over from *Panorama* to view it and arrangements were made for extracts to be shown and for Peter Lemass to fly to London to appear in the Panorama programme. Unfortunately the programme was cancelled at the last minute because the Federal Nigerian government refused to supply a spokesman and the BBC would not proceed without one. The film is now of historical interest. Extracts are being used in a BBC programme for showing in 1986 or 1987.

Brazil

It is probably easier nowadays, but in 1977 Brazil was a difficult place to film. Foreign crews tended to be harassed, and have their film confiscated when they were found filming in shanty towns or other politically sensitive areas. The name of Archbishop Helder Camara could not be mentioned in the Brazilian media, to say nothing of his utterances!

The trip to Brazil was the first attempt by Radharc to tackle the subjects of liberation theology and basic christian communities, which have since become so important in the life of the Latin American Church. Tom Stack was perhaps the prime instigator of the project, Dermod McCarthy the Director. Between them they produced five programmes, of which I think three were important. *The Earth Belongs to Everyone* brought Helder Camara for the first time to the Irish screen — the man who once said that the church should be the voice of the voiceless. *New Day in Brazil*

67

looked at basic christian communities. But the film which proved to be the most important was an unpretentious report on a meeting of the Brazilian bishops called *These Men are dangerous*. This was eventually shown in full or in part in many countries, and a high level attempt was made — unsuccessful I think — to show it to the Pope before his first visit to Brazil. The importance of this film lay in the spelling out by radical members of the Brazilian hierarchy of what the option for the poor and the gospel of liberation really meant for the Church.

Tom O'Dea, television critic in the Irish Press, wrote a longish piece on the series at the time.

> What message then did Radharc bring back? . . . It is the gospel of self reliance, for a start, and it is the antithesis of the Irish historical approach, which was protectionist and which willy nilly built up a dependency and a subservience.
>
> The church as Radharc projects it now, wishes its people to have thews and sinews, and Radharc is pointing the finger at the Irish Church and intimating that a better model can be found elsewhere . . .
>
> All the time throughout the whole series Radharc seemed to be looking at the map of Brazil on a transparent screen and to be seeing Ireland clearly through it.
>
> I think it would not be overstating the matter one whit to say that Radharc went to Brazil to show us Ireland. It is a simple paradox which Radharc — now a fairly sophisticated operation — is capable of incorporating in its technique.

Tom O'Dea has a reputation as a perceptive tough journalist. If I quote him it is perhaps because I would like to think that what he says is true. However, one would have to be honest and say that there are still other reasons for filming abroad, despite the difficulties and discomforts.

For one thing it is easier to speak with independence about a foreign church. At home one knows too many people who are likely to be hurt by the truth, and are near enough to make that hurt known. Then again, one asks somebody for an interview in Ireland and they say, "Well this week is out, and the following week would be difficult – what about early next month?" If we were a foreign team in Ireland they would know it has to be done tomorrow, if not today.

At home too there are so many other things to occupy one's mind: letters, enquiries, problems about work in progress; it's so

68

easy to put off shooting to tomorrow, even if it is only because the weather may be better! But away from home there are few distractions and a kind of fury for work takes hold, which may be tiring at the time, but very productive in the end result.

Central America

In our film on Nicaragua, *The Exemplary Revolution*, we included a piece of stock footage showing an American TV journalist being shot dead in cold blood by a soldier of President Somoza. One could see him lying on the road. One could see the soldier waving his gun threateningly at him. One could see his head jerk in the air as the bullet hit him.

A whole television crew from Holland were murdered in El Salvador. There wasn't any film made of their deaths. Dutch television can't do programmes in Central America now because nobody will give them insurance. Thirty priests and religious have been murdered in Guatemala since 1981. The rate was one a month in the early 1980's. Forty-nine journalists were assassinated in 1980-81. Twenty-seven staff and fifty students were killed in the National University in 1980. A bishop closed down the diocese of El Quiche for two and a half years because he felt the Church could not continue to operate when so many of its personnel were killed or under threat of being killed.

And then there is the murder of Archbishop Oscar Arnulfo Romero, Archbishop of San Salvador, shot in the heart at the consecration of the Mass. And twelve of his priests.

We've seen some violence in Northern Ireland but I don't remember any journalist or cameraman being shot. Nor has it been common to murder clergymen.

Filming alone

The ways and means of making public affairs documentary film alone is one area of film in which I profess to be more knowledgeable than most other film makers — perhaps because nobody else is fool enough to try.

It's a tough game, and I don't recommend it to people who want to see their children's children. I have only tried it in two kinds of situations. The first was where I had no hope of getting permission to film, let alone bring a crew, as in the refugee camps in Thailand; the second was in El Salvador, Nicaragua and Guatemala where one can feel freer to accept possible dangers in a situation when one is not responsible for others with mothers, wives and children.

One man film crews only became possible within the last ten years and one instrument in particular made it possible — the Nagra SN Recorder. This recorder is about the size of two packets of cigarettes. Despite its size it has a frequency response equal to the best available in the professional field. And just as important, it runs for forty minutes on tiny spools of tape which means that it's possible to carry enough tapes to cover a month of filming within a very small package.

Filming alone of course is to some extent a misnomer. One has to look for a helper, be it for an hour or a day or a week. This can work very well if one finds an intelligent person who can speak the local language *and* English and who knows his or her way around. One then has a guide and interpreter as well as a helper and friend.

A range of techniques is possible when interviewing:

1. The film producer/cameraman may interview from the camera and ask the subject to talk to him through the lens. (I used this technique in Nicaragua.)
2. The camera may be set on a wide shot of the interviewee. The producer then moves to the side, switches on the camera and conducts the interview as would an ordinary interviewer. This entails keeping a sharp eye on the subject lest he or she move from the opening position, which would necessitate stopping the interview and reframing the subject. Alternatively, the camera may be set for a two-handed interview, as on a park bench.
3. A helpful intelligent friend may be briefed on how to put a few agreed questions to the interviewee,
   or the producer/cameraman may conduct the interview, but ask the subject to address his answers to the helpful friend.

   The recorder itself may be run on automatic level control or monitored from the camera.

Thailand

It was the time when the Vietnamese boat people were turning up all over Asia and their awful plight had caught the imagination of television audiences around the world.

I didn't feel there was much that we could add to the television coverage of the boat people. But there was another refugee story

70

That's fine. Now just relax while I ask you a few questions.

that wasn't being told — the story of Hmong and Laotians trying to escape into Thailand and being hunted down by Vietnamese troops. Estimates suggested that 140,000 were already locked into camps along the Thai border. Nobody wanted them, so their temporary accommodation was acquiring all the signs of being permanent.

I was advised that there was little point in asking the Thai government to facilitate a television crew. The media were giving them enough trouble over the boat people, and for the rest let sleeping dogs lie. So I decided to go alone and try without permission.

Friends in Bangkok put me in touch with a Phillipino lady doctor who worked in one of the camps and was agreeable to try and help. She got me into the main camp and put out the story that I was taking photographs to illustrate her medical work.

I filmed a little around her wooden hospital and it didn't cause problems. There was a young boy who had been shot in the leg and now it had gone gangrenous. He was old enough to know what that meant and yet was brave. A few days later he lost the leg.

I interviewed a girl of about thirteen or fourteen. Her name sounded like Chu Yang — she was a refugee who had come through Laos with her family from Vietnam. She had lost her mother and father in an ambush near the Thai border and didn't know whether they were dead or alive. She had been waiting eleven days to be operated on for the removal of a bullet in her left lung.

Many of the people escaping through Laos to Thailand were Hmong. The Hmong are a tribe of Chinese origin who had lived for some hundreds of years in Vietnam. At this time there were

71

tense relations between China and Vietnam and the Hmong suffered as a result.

At a camp beside the river which forms the border between Laos and Thailand I met two families of Hmong who had crossed the previous night. They had several young children who appeared to be in a deep sleep. Escaping families cannot risk having their position disclosed by crying children. So the children are given heavy doses of opium during the journey. Many of them arrive in Thailand with all the symptoms of drug addiction — even before they can walk.

The next day the doctor brought me to a kind of corral-like structure some miles away where new arrivals were processed. Here we were refused permission to enter with a camera. So we went away and came back later when there were different guards on the gate, one of whom the doctor knew. We got in this time but it was a fight against the clock. She was nervous and wanted things done quickly. But I needed a lot of footage and there were plenty of potential pictures literally lying around — thousands of people crowded together with no proper facilities, whole families living in the corner of a balcony or even in hollowed out areas under buildings. One tap supplied hundreds of people.

She showed me the few toilets overflowing with excreta and maggots and I filmed — millions of maggots. I just kept going until eventually she felt our luck couldn't stretch any further. So we beat a hasty retreat.

The next day in the main camp I went for broke. Filmed like mad and tried to do as much as I could before I was stopped. After about an hour or two I heard the camp loudspeaker system spring into life with a rather insistent message. It wasn't long before somebody who knew both Thai and English came over to me to tell me to proceed at once to the guardhouse at the front gate. I ran to the hospital and fortunately found the doctor at home. She had been busy and had heard nothing. "Lie low," she said, "and I'll go to the gate." Some money or favour must have passed over, but anyway when she came back the matter had been dealt with — I would not have to face a military court. But the camera must remain in its case until I got to Bangkok.

The programme about the refugees was completed in 1979 and called *Escape to Nowhere*. But the visit also produced four other films. *The Angels of Bangkok* dealt with the work of Irish Sisters trying to help young girls caught up in the prostitution racket. *Blue Eyes and Saffron Robes, Have a Happy Rebirth*, and *It's Meant to be Boring* concentrated on different aspects of Buddhism.

One of the more surprising aspects of the trip was to find a number of relatively young Europeans and Americans living as monks in forest monasteries in remote parts of Thailand. One I visited had an abbot who was a veteran of the Vietnam war. His community included a science graduate from London University, a former student of the English Benedictines, and an ex-hippy who had rolled in some months before and just decided to stay. They lived on one meal a day. This was gathered in the local village where they went every morning with begging bowls. They ate whatever the local people in their goodness put into it, mixed up together, which might include savoury rice from one and chocolate sauce from another. They all had, or had had dysentery and hepatitis. In fact, I got my introduction to them from one of their number, a young Englishman of Irish descent called Sean who was down attending the Buddhist hospital in Bangkok – staffed only by male nurses! I also met a French catholic priest in another forest monastery. When I asked him about saying Mass during an interview on camera he smiled, made negative gestures with his hand out of picture, and waited for the next question.

Guatemala

One of the bleaker moments in my life was arriving alone in Guatemala airport. Airline rules with regard to hand luggage allow one bag, reading matter and a camera. My one bag contained extra magazines for the camera, head for the tripod, and sound equipment. Weight approx 30 lbs. I also had reading matter in the form of all my papers and research material, plus breviary, passport, tickets, reading glasses — in a plastic bag. And a camera. The camera was an Arriflex SR2 weight 29 lbs. Total hand luggage over 60 lbs.

I collected my other luggage off the ramp. It consisted of a tripod, weight 14 lbs, 40 cans of film weight 65 lbs, and a small bag of personal belongings with bits and pieces of equipment, 15 lbs. 94 lbs altogether. I was tired after a hard fortnight in Grenada and had had to come a very roundabout way to get to Guatemala, through Trinidad, Curacao, and San José. It took about twenty hours with two changes of airline. Fortunately there wasn't too much hassle at customs.

When planning the trip I had reasonable hope of being able to pick up an Irish missioner in San Salvador who would show me the ropes in Guatemala. So I had booked a ticket accordingly. It was only in Grenada that I could finally confirm that they were too short staffed to spare anybody. Instead they had asked a sister in Guatemala city to help me. I should phone her on arrival.

Perhaps because it was Sunday evening I couldn't find a porter. Ferrying the equipment over to the phone booth which seemed to be the other end of the airport meant carrying it in several stages. Which also meant leaving baggage unattended for short periods, and therefore pilferable. It's a risk one has to take when one is alone.

When I phoned the nun, she was out. In fact, all the nuns in the small community were out, and there was only a local girl on the phone who didn't understand my Spanish patois. And if she said anything useful I'm afraid I didn't understand it either. So I put down the phone and thought about plan B.

I'd heard the Maryknoll Fathers had a house in Guatemala City so I asked about the Padres Maryknoll. Nobody seemed to have heard of them. So I took up the phone book. I looked up Maryknoll, Religious Houses, Churches, anything I could think of. The only Maryknoll entry looked a bit suspicious, and when I phoned there was no answer. I wrote down the address — faut de mieux; hailed a taxi and climbed in with all my 154 lbs of delicate baggage. The taximan brought me to the centre of Guatemala city where he drew up outside a shop called Maryknoll. It looked like there had been a closing down sale some six months before.

So I sent the taximan to find a phone, call up the convent again and find out how to get there. I had a new plan. When we got to the convent I asked where the phone was, and found close by what I was looking for — a church guide to Guatemala. After that there was no problem in finding the Maryknoll Fathers. The irony of it was that their house was about five minutes from the airport, while the convent was on the other side of Guatemala city.

Now the sister I was to contact was out of town for a week. So here I was in Guatemala city, equipped and ready to make a film about the church in Guatemala, without contact or guide. I got to bed early, had one of the best night's sleep since I had left Ireland, and was in the library next morning at 9 o'clock.

One of the big advantages of being in a religious house is that they always have a library, and the library usually has recent and back issues of the local newspapers, religious periodicals and magazines, as well as sections on history, culture etc. So anything one might be interested in with respect to the state of religion in the country is likely to be found somewhere.

One doesn't stay in the library however, one takes books and magazines out to the commonroom where there's a fridge and a cold drink and comfortable chairs. People come to the library to read rather than to talk. I needed to read *and* talk to people.

I learnt a fair bit that day about the awful state of Guatemala and met a number of visitors. But none seemed to offer any opening to get started. Then came supper. A new priest appeared on the scene. Fr. Jan, it appeared, performed some peculiar mission up country. I sat beside him, and listened. He had a truck and was down doing messages in Guatemala city. He would be going up country tomorrow to Coban, where the bishop was having a week's seminar dealing with pastoral matters in the diocese.

A car going up country to the Alta Vera Paz! A bishop collecting his priests, nuns and lay helpers into one place where one could meet everybody, make contacts and find out what was going on! It was too good to be true. So I pleaded with him to take me along, and he agreed, if reluctantly.

The Alta Vera Paz.

Next morning when he saw all the luggage, I think he would have excused himself if he could, but I made sure not to leave him an opportunity. Admittedly the van was smaller than I had imagined and I ended up with the camera and accessory bag (total weight 59 lb) on my knee — protesting that I was quite comfortable. I may have been then, but my body ached a long time before we reached our destination, Coban, some hours later.

On the way we passed several army checkpoints but these didn't trouble Jan and Jan covered me. I learnt afterwards that, because of his Hungarian origins he was naturally very anti-Communist and anti-anything with left wing associations. He ran a medical mission, which was medical and, it was said, very little mission. He made a reasonable living from his medical practice and had a close friendship with the army in his area who frequently gave him lifts in helicopters and so on. This made other priests suspicious.

He had prostrate trouble, which meant that we stopped often, which was fortunate because the scenery was beautiful and I needed to get the camera off my knee.

The meeting was held at the seminary in Coban which was also a religious house of American Benedictines. Despite the fact that they had this big conference on their hands, and that I came unannounced, they gave me a welcome and food at their table. I was now in an ideal situation to meet and talk to people and interview anyone of interest. Which included the Bishop — an intelligent and good man who had not been afraid to stick his neck out in the cause of justice.

The Army

A film about Central America without pictures of the army would be like a film about hell which left out the devil. I first came across the problem in El Salvador where I was staying with the Irish Franciscans up country in Gotera. They knew the army people and asked on my behalf but I was refused permission. This was a very serious situation. However, shortly afterwards the annual fiesta took place in Gotera. This meant a lot of people coming in to town and a lot of entertainment. Crowds have to be watched in El Salvador, so the army came out in force and when they did, I took their picture — while pretending to film the entertainment.

In Coban, Guatemala, I didn't bother asking the army for permission but sat in a landrover outside their base. The camera was covered by a dark shirt and the eye piece turned in such a way that I seemed to be looking the opposite direction to the filming. I got no useful footage. Very little army traffic came in or out of the base and what did come tended to go the opposite way to what I expected. So I gave up after forty minutes. The parked landrover was becoming too conspicuous.

The next day there were preparations under way for a cycle marathon passing through town and that gave me a new idea. Outside the main civic building they put up a platform and a microphone. Some local radio DJ representing the sponsors of the rally was trying to pep up local interest — giving up-to-date information about the position of the riders and many other such things of interest to cycling afficianados. And being in Spanish, of course, it took a long time. So I set up nonchalantly in front of the stand hoping to pass as cameraman for some local TV station. But I kept my powder dry and prayed that the army might arrive and give a little exhibition of themselves.

Presumably because it helps to terrorise the peasants, the Guatemalan army regularly rush around in jeeps, pulling up in a flurry wherever there is a crowd. A few officers and a load of conscripts jump out, take up firing positions and wave their guns in the direction of potential enemies. After a few minutes they all file back again and chase off somewhere else.

Well it worked like a dream. I wasn't there ten minutes when they pulled up nearly in front of the camera. There was a full load of film and I just let it run. The young soldiers looked at me uncertainly but I think the disguise worked. Nobody shouted stop and nobody pulled a trigger. (If you'd heard the first-hand stories that I had heard in the previous week, you too might have considered the latter a possibility.)

The Civil Patrol

One of the more diabolical acts of the army in Guatemala is to force illiterate peasants into a kind of citizens army, called the Civil Patrol. Part of their duties is to set up road blocks and check traffic, guard installations etc. I was told that if they were guarding a bridge and the bridge was blown up, the guards were killed. If they guarded a power station and the power station was blown up thirty members of the local civil patrol would be killed. Which helps to explain why they have a reputation for shooting first and asking questions afterwards.

I was in Northern Guatemala on the tourist road to Tikal, one of the ancient Mayan cities, when we were stopped at a checkpoint by one of these patrols. There was a car just beyond the checkpoint riddled with bullets. The brother with me told me that it had been shot up a few days before, that the owner lived just down the road, and that he must have been well known to the people who shot him.

So how do you film the Civil Patrol without becoming a martyr to television? A quiet little American Benedictine brother showed me how. We cruised around in the landrover outside a town about 20 miles from base until he spotted somebody he knew, some minor local official. We were within shooting (sic) distance of a civil patrol checkpoint so he hopped out, told me to get the camera up, engaged this minor official in pleasant conversation and told me to be quick and get the pictures.

So I set up as if to film the brother and friend and filmed the checkpoint instead. The three guys with guns were a bit unsure of what I was at, and what they should do about it, but the presence of the local official seemed to confuse them enough for me to get the pictures and hop back into the landrover before they could come to a decision.

The film was eventually called *Where the Pope is a Communist and the Bishop a Guerrilla,* an echo of the sentiments of a Guatemalan landowner quoted in the film. It was forty minutes long and a difficult film to make. I felt that if RTÉ rather than Radharc/RTÉ had come back from Guatemala with film, it might have made the front page of the RTÉ Guide. But even though I sent in an article in good time, and some good photos, I was upset to find that nothing was published. I hoped I might recover a bit by getting the programme mentioned on one of the morning radio shows, but although I left a pleading letter on the producer's desk, there was no mention. None of the critics noticed it either. I hoped Trócaire might become interested in distributing video copies, but they lost interest in Radharc when a bishop criticised them in an earlier film about Grenada. So I was disappointed. The only control on subversive US activity in Central America is international public opinion. I think our films on El Salvador and Nicaragua have helped to alert public opinion in Ireland to the situation in these countries — by being broadcast in the first place, but also through many showings on film and video, mostly organised through Trócaire. The film about Guatemala, however, perhaps the country which most needs the focus of international attention, sank without trace.*

Nicaragua

Having completed a film in El Salvador in 1979, I thought I'd try my hand at getting into Nicaragua. This was less than six months after the revolution. One of the Irish Franciscans came down with me to San Salvador and we tried the Nicaraguan Embassy. The

---

*Footnote

Since writing the above, the Guatemala programme received one of five equal awards made at the Christian TV Week, held this year in Mainz, West Germany. What this means in simple terms is that it was chosen as one of the five best programmes of Christian interest produced anywhere in the world during the past three years.

place seemed to be run by three or four teenage gunmen who lolled around swinging their machine guns. They said it was closed. We went back and consulted a travel agent friend of one of the priests. I remember a gorgeous girl, full of laughter, vitality and helpfulness. She phoned the embassy, introduced herself with the words, "la Patria o morir" (the fatherland or death) accompanied by a big wink in our direction. This was for the sake of the teenage revolutionary heroes. She then asked for the ambassador. The ambassador eventually came to the phone and said that if we came about four o'clock he'd give me papers. So I arrived at four and strolled nonchalently pass the gunmen.

The little ambassador and his wife, who were obviously left over from the previous regime, and were trying to make the best of having half a dozen gun-toting cuckoos in their nest, typed up all the documents in quadruplicate — under military surveillance. And so off to Managua.

"La patria o morir."

Manuaga is a bit like the photographs of Hiroshima after the Atomic bomb, except the square patches between the roads are green. There was an earthquake there in 1972 and most of it was never rebuilt. It's said the relief money collected was swallowed up by President Somoza's family and friends.

I'd been given the name of a house belonging to an order of priests who shall be nameless, so I got a car from the airport and arrived at their doorstep with all my bags and equipment. They were mostly Americans. I told them what I hoped to do and asked them to suggest somewhere I might stay, expecting they would say, "here". But they didn't. They suggested the Hilton, which I could not afford, or failing that a small private hotel close by.

The private hotel was really a restaurant of the Chinese sort, with a room behind the restaurant — very hot, badly lit and badly ventilated.

This is the only case I can remember where a shared priesthood failed to guarantee hospitality.

So there I was in a strange city knowing nobody, sharing a corrugated cabin with cockroaches and mosquitoes, in a city where there was nothing to buy, hardly anywhere to go, and a telephone system which would make An Bord Telecom look like Ma Bell.

To further complicate things, the names of the roads had been changed since the revolution mostly because they were called after the friends of the hated Somoza. So it was very difficult to find an address. Addresses were relative to some landmark, six blocks south and four blocks east of the Church of St Barbara or some such designation.

It took a whole miserable week before I could get going. But eventually I got on the track of an Amercian nun who lived in a poor suburb with a friend of hers, another American whose husband had been killed in the revolution. This nun was rumoured to be very well connected with the new powers that be. But she was very busy. Now I knew it was difficult to live in Managua at that period; nobody had any money. Somaza had sent his son with a posse armed with machine guns to go around the banks and strip them of cash and valuables before leaving for Miami. So I offered a cold business deal. She would get me a young university student with English to guide me around Nicaragua. She would arrange interviews for me with important people. In return I would give her a substantial sum of money in dollars. It worked like a dream. Within a few days she arranged interviews with the foreign minister, Miguel d'Escoto, the minister in charge of literacy, Roberto Cardenal, the minister of agriculture and land reform, Jaime Wheelock, and several others.

I also asked her to arrange for me to take photos of the army. This entailed going to what was called "the bunker" which had previously been the Somoza HQ. We were put in a room with a number of waiting journalists. They all had requests, and most of them seemed to be turned down.

Then my student friend's turn came and he went forward and talked to the army officer. I could see that he wasn't getting very far, so I nipped up and whispered to him, "Show him the note from Sister Mary. Show him the note from Sr. Mary." He pulled the crumpled bit of paper out of his pocket and handed it to the officer. Immediately the atmosphere changed. We were shown into

The president has decided that you should re-invest in Miami.

a separate room while the others were summarily dealt with. The officer then came in ready to do our bidding. Everything was possible. The troops marched up and down before us and we were shown the most advantageous places for shots. The young student who within a few days had seen a lot of places and met a lot of people whom he never expected to meet or see in a lifetime, turned to me and said with wondering eyes, "That Sister Mary sure knows a lot of people."

Interviewing Jaime Wheelock, Minister for Land Reform, was quite an experience. We arrived as per appointment at three o'clock at his office to hear that he had been called out on urgent business. I gathered afterwards from other sources that some of the peasants who thought that they would become landowners after the revolution, were a little upset to find that they were only to become proud members of a cooperative. Much pouring of oil on troubled waters was apparently required of the Minister for Land Reform at this stage of the revolution.

I was determined to get him if possible, so I hummed and hawed and said I'd be quite happy to wait. We hung around for about an hour and a half. Then the door burst open and in marched Wheelock in uniform bristling with revolvers and surrounded by a bodyguard of four alert young men with machine guns. I thought of Michael Collins. He was disconcerted to find me there and not all that gruntled. "It will only take a few minutes," I pleaded, "I'll set up outside and we'll call you." So he reluctantly agreed.

I set up in a hollow out of the breeze and sent in a message. Again he swept out with the four bodyguards who stationed themselves north, south, east and west on the higher ground overlooking us. After the interview was over, he thawed out a bit and asked about the situation in Ireland, and showed more knowledge of Ireland and its history than one might expect your average Irish politician to have about Nicaragua.

13

Permissions

We rarely ask for permission to film in a country. One of the few exceptions was South Africa; we felt we mightn't get away without it. Another factor influencing the decision was some off-the-record information from a film manufacturer to the effect that their branch in South Africa was under instructions to inform the government of anybody who bought professional cine film.

Peter Lemass made the request. He was refused permission. No reason was given.

Apart from South Africa, India and Russia, I can't remember that we ever sought permission. Most countries don't mind, or if they do mind, there's not much point in asking them because they will probably say no. Why risk a negative answer when one will probably get away with it if one is reasonably careful?

Guatemala for instance has a system of licensing journalists. But the government of Guatemala has so much to hide there seems little point in asking them for the press card.

These modern videos, which are camera and recorder combined into one bulky package, are a godsend to TV cameramen on the prowl. The amateur instrument looks very little different from the professional film camera so a cameraman can pass himself off as a wealthy tourist. It's only when he has to team up with a sound man waving one of these big sausage mikes that danger may threaten. Headphones and rifle mikes are more symbolic of TV than any camera. So a very discreet soundman is essential if a cameraman is to escape official attention.

If I am worried about being questioned in a country about

permission to film I try to avoid the larger towns and especially the capital city. For some reason I don't understand policemen and others in the capital seem more inclined to stop one and ask questions. Two of us were nearly arrested in Jakarta, Indonesia, because we could not produce written permission. We bluffed our way out of that one — pretended to be tourists doing a video. But most of the time in Jakarta we had to be covered by a helpful local journalist who showed his official press card whenever we were challenged by suspicious policemen.

Russia
In 1978 Tom Stack and I went on an exploratory trip to Moscow and Leningrad and made tentative arrangements to film a story on the Orthodox Church. Normally we can't afford this preliminary reconnaissance trip but I knew we would have to have advance permission for *everything* in Russia (which is a great disadvantage in documentary filming, where the story tends to grow and one thing leads to another).

The office of the Patriarch in Moscow, for instance, suggested that we visit the seminary in Zagorsk, forty kilometres outside Moscow. We would be driven there in the Patriarch's car, by his driver (a member of the KGB) and his interpreter. But Zagorsk wasn't on our original itinerary, so it took about a week to get the necessary clearance from the government.

Travelling to Zagorsk in the car, we tried to talk to the interpreter but he made signs in the direction of the driver, which were calculated to shut us up. Eventually he did talk to us — out in the middle of a field near the monastery. And after we had had our talk, he asked would we like a smoke (smoking is forbidden

at the monastery of Zagorsk). We said we would, so he brought us into the lavatory, where we stood, four in a row facing the open cubicles, and partook of a hasty drag. It reminded me of the old days in Maynooth.

Back in Moscow we met the late Patrick O'Donovan, the English journalist, wandering around the Kremlin. He was over to cover a visit of the Archbishop of Canterbury for the *Observer*, but the newspapers had forgotten to put Kiev on his itinerary. So when the Archbishop went off to Kiev, Patrick had to stay in Moscow, because that is all his travel documents permitted.

We succeeded in talking to some dissidents, though it wasn't easy. Igor Shafarevich, mathematician and friend of Zacharov, was an intelligent good man whom one would love to have interviewed on film. I remember well his comment on our remark that the Orthodox churches only seemed to be patronised by the old, and what would happen when the old passed on? "When I was a boy", he said, "people were saying the same thing".

A supposedly secret visit to the late Boris Pasternak's son was complicated by the attentions of an official driver — all of them are minor agents of the KGB. As we called a taxi he appeared from nowhere, and climbed in, despite protests. He didn't leave until he found out where we were going, which of course we couldn't conceal because we had to give instructions to the taxi driver. The only rational explanation of why he followed us that night was that somebody had been listening to our conversation earlier in the evening when it would have been clear that we were up to some mischief, though unclear exactly what. The fact that every room where foreigners in Moscow are likely to congregate is bugged by the KGB is an accepted fact of life in the diplomatic community in Moscow.

When we arrived Pasternak greeted us with gestures to indicate that the walls had ears. Among other things we talked about his father whose letters he was editing at the time; he spoke English well enough to correct my grammar gently on one occasion.

When we were leaving I asked him if we could do anything for him. He thought for a moment, and said, "I am translating the works of C S Lewis into Russian, and I am missing some volumes." So we promised to try and help. All but two were traced through Foyles of London, and dispatched by a complicated route. I know he got them because I checked, but how he got them is a diplomatic secret!

It was a number of such incidents that made me funk the effort of trying to make documentary film in Russia. Which may have been the Government's general intention.

India

The most troublesome country we ever filmed in was India. Before visas would be issued, a detailed summary of subject matter, list of persons to be interviewed, places to be visited had to be submitted. This, it was explained to us, was necessary because each State had to be informed of our project, in order to be able to provide somebody to accompany us. Normally the film company paid for this attendant, but in our case the cost would be waived because we were making a film for an Irish development agency. Unfortunately the film required a lot of travel, and every time we crossed a state border we had to visit the state capital, introduce ourselves to the local Minister of Information and ask for the pleasure of having somebody to accompany us whom we didn't want or need.

One of our film locations was a fisheries co-op near Trivandrum. The gentleman who accompanied us each day was proud of the fact that he had been trained for six months in Moscow and always carried a gun. He confided after a few drinks to some of the Indians that were working with us that he had us watched night *and* day!

I remember being sorry for another Indian gentleman who happened to be on his holidays and was brought back from a great distance to attend us in our brief visit to his State, where we photographed a few prize cattle.

Sixteen million people travel by train every day in India. At night the seats turn into beds, and provided one can sleep happily in trains, it's possible to wake every day in a different Indian state without wasting time or money.

Sometimes we got the impression that one or other persons booked into our carriage knew more about us than they pretended. But that could be par for the course. All foreigners are watched in India.

Priests in one parish where we stayed admitted that they knew which beggars at the gate were paid to watch their movements. Foreigners may not move freely around India without informing the police. One priest told us of slipping up to Hyderabad to do a little shopping. One week later he met the local police chief who waggled his finger and said, 'Ah ha father, you were in Hyderabad, and you never told me.' The experience of India helped to explain how a small band of mongols or moguls could come in from outside and rule many millions of people. And to explain how a few British could come some centuries later and take over control. It takes very few to rule a country, provided they know everything that is going on.

14

There's a price to be paid for everything

Mosquitoes

It's unfortunate that many of the most interesting places in the world to visit are also visited by the malarial mosquito. Mosquitoes like new blood and go for the visitor before the local resident. There are pills to take which protect one against malaria. I tend not to take them if I can avoid it because I was told they can affect the eyesight. That may be an old wives' tale but I don't wish to find out that it isn't.

There are various other precautions to be taken against the mosquito. One of the cheapest and most universal is a green coil, said to be made of cow dung and chemicals. When lit by a match, it burns slowly giving off smoke. All that's left in the morning is the metal holder and a spiral of ash. While you breathe acrid fumes all night, the mosquitoes take a whiff and wisely clear out.

I read once about a device in the *Sunday Times* small ads and sent off £9 immediately to buy one. The principle sounded clever. A little box produces an electronic noise, the ad said, which mimics the sound made by some dangerous enemy of the mosquito. So they clear off. That was the theory anyway.

The box indeed buzzed. But the mosquitoes paid not the slightest attention and continued to bite and suck with the usual gay abandon.

Mosquito nets are the traditional protection, but in my experience it's very rare to find one without holes. And it is quite uncanny how a mosquito can find the smallest tear in the netting to enter. First night in any place, as a matter of course, I examine the net if one is provided. Wherever there are holes or tears, I apply camera tape — and remove it before leaving in case the host might object.

Malaria is one of the greatest scourges of the human race. Probably more so than famine because it affects so many more people. In the late fifties and sixties it looked like it might be wiped out. Alas, when the new independent countries ran short of cash, they diverted money from eradication programmes. Since then malaria has been on the increase.

Inevitably one finds oneself in places where little can be done to counter the mosquito, except to get the job done fast and get out.

Accommodation for the visitor to Fr Bede Griffith's ashram, on the banks of the Cauvery River in South India, was a tiny room with a concrete shelf and an open windowless window. One slept on the shelf in a cloud of insects. I never saw a crew so anxious to finish the job and get out quickly.

Injections

It is geneally accepted nowadays that the risk of getting smallpox is smaller than the risk of getting an injection against smallpox. So many countries don't require immunisation any more.

By the 1970s, the disease had virtually disappeared, although certificates of vaccination were still required. My doctor didn't consider immunisation wise or necessary so he gave me a bogus vaccination with a wink and a nod. My chances of meeting smallpox, he said, were negligible.

A month later we were filming at a grass church in open country. We took off part of the roof and all of one side to let in the light. I thought of the gospel story where the roof was removed to let down the paralytic.

During the Mass there was a persistent din from a village about a mile away — the land being flat, noise travelled far. We were curious to find out what was happening, so when we had finished we climbed into the landrovers and headed cross country.

There were at least a hundred people sitting around the village. Most of them had gallon cans, which were being refilled from large oil drums. They contained native beer. We were told that the daughter of the head man in the village had died. In Irish terms, we were attending the wake.

Brian O'Reilly took a few pictures, while we were introduced to the chief and everybody shook his hand. I asked the missionary to enquire how the daughter had died. The answer came back quickly, Smallpox!

It was an hour's drive home. I kept my right hand out the window and so did Billy Fitzgerald; and when we got home we plunged them into disinfectant.

Cholera on the other hand, we met quite often. Sometimes we picked victims off the road and slung them in the back of the landrover, dropping them off at the hospital on the way. At the time I thought we were brave, but in fact cholera is rarely passed on by contact. It's a water borne disease.

Dysentery is caught from uncooked food and bad water and it's easy to catch if one is not careful. Canned or bottled drinks are obviously safe but one has to make sure they are not served with ice, which may have been made with contaminated water. Peter Lemass and Des Forristal got dysentery in the Philippines. Des had trouble from it for years afterwards.

Peter was dropped off in Cebu where his stay in hospital was memorable for many reasons, not all of them printable. Half the patients in his ward were recovering from knife wounds. Elsewhere we were introduced to a man on a Cursillo who publicly confessed to committing twenty murders. We all shook his hand and congratulated him on his conversion. The Philippines was, and is, a violent society.

Another interesting patient in Peter's hospital was under strong sedation. He had been put under the evil eye, and believed he would die within twenty-four hours. If nothing had been done he would have died. But the relatives brought him to hospital and had him put to sleep for thirty-six hours. When he woke up and realised that the time had passed, and he was still alive, he resumed normal living.

Water and the lack of it

Water on tap is a luxury and a blessing which nobody but nobody in the first world appreciates. While the Irish man or woman turns on a tap, others dig a deep hole in the earth and hope some dirty brown liquid may seep into it. And even when there are pipes and taps in third world countries, one has no guarantee that they can deliver — now, tomorrow or even next week.

I rememer Cotobato in the Philippines for different reasons. When we arrived at the grass strip airport, a banner greeted us with the legend, "Cock fights every night of the week in honour of the Immaculate Conception by courtesy of Pepsi Cola".

There was a school concert at the stadium one afternoon and

90

for some reason we felt obliged to attend. The brass band played all the works of Tchaikovski in five minutes which caused Des Forristal to suffer uncontrollable convulsions of laughter which were not only embarrassing but quite worrying. Then the heavens opened and the concert was suspended. As we sheltered waiting for the break, I noted some naked children dancing happily in a deluge of water pouring off the edge of the roof.

Suddenly the rain stopped and we made a dash for the van. It was only a small jump across the ditch, but my foot slipped on take-off and I missed the other bank. When the statutory period of merriment — in which I didn't join — was over, it took several people to haul me out. I was in liquid mud up to the top of my trousers.

Since most of the population of Cotobato city relieve themselves openly into these ditches, or should I say sewers, the smell off the liquid mud was abominable and the health hazard unthinkable.

I arrived in the back of an open truck at the bishop's house where we were staying, went up the back stairs leaving as little mess as possible, threw off everything, got into the shower and turned on the tap. There was no water and there would not be any until next morning. If the rain hadn't stopped I would have joined the kids under the eaves, and hang the modesty.

Customs

I know they are a necessary evil but I just hate customs. "Isn't it wonderful?" people say to you, going off to all those interesting places. Well it's not at all wonderful, when you arrive with sixty cans of film worth £3,000, a recorder worth £5,000 and a camera worth £20,000. There are no rules. Each time it's different.

How I love Argentina! The Irish Dominican Sisters ran a school there, and one of their ex-students worked for the airline which brought us to Buenos Aires. She had been tipped off, and as we came out of the plane she took us by the hand and wafted us through passport control, which was OK, and gave a nod and a wink at the customs officer and waived us through customs, which was wonderful.

Alas, it's not normally like that.

If I ever meet John Paul II, I hope it will be somewhere passing through customs. Customs men never find me without a collar. A Catholic priest with a camera who makes little films is a lot less threatening than a television crew working for a national broadcasting agency. A simple-minded man of the cloth may be

91

forgiven for not understanding all the complications of international exchange and trade. It doesn't work all the time but I've never known it to be a hindrance.

Sometimes a deposit is required. And in any well-run country this is not a great problem. One produces a credit card and signs away a lot of money. However, it's all collectable when one leaves the country. Usually anyway. We did have an interesting argument once with the customs in Nairobi; they had insisted on a large down payment — perhaps £1,000 in modern money. However, it would all be collectable upon our exit, or so we were promised. So come the time to leave, we were at the airport early and presented the equipment as proof that we hadn't sold anything, and claimed back the deposit. Were we proposing to take the money out of the country? Of course we were. Well that was unfortunate because the money could only be given to us in the form of Kenyan shillings which could only be spent in Kenya!

Which reminds me of the time when the police were summoned to put me in jail in Zanzibar because I refused to pay for a room with a bath. There was no dispute with the management over the facts — both of us agreed there was a bath adjoining and that the bath was not connected to the water supply. The only dispute arose as to whether I should pay for a bath which didn't, so to speak, bathe.

A delicate crisis of conscience can arise when the customs stall and it's quite clear that they're waiting for, shall we say, a little gift. I can remember sitting it out for an hour and a half in one West Indian Country, until the customs officer let us go in disgust. It was time for him to go home!

For a trouble-free exit from Indonesia, we were reliably informed, there were certain set procedures which we would disregard at our peril. There was an acceptable figure for each bag, which one left openly if not ostentatiously on top of the carrying handle.

Cuba, as one might expect, was different. We were guests of the Ministry of Information, and were told that we would be met at the airport by an official of the Ministry. Well no official in fact appeared and we were very much at the mercy of the customs.

Had we any papers or films? Well, we'd no papers but we had a lot of film (probably liable to appalling duties, I thought glumly). A tin of film was produced and the customs man proceeded to try and open it. Hurried explanations that the film was unexposed and . . . Unexposed? Immediately he lost interest, and waived us through. Whereas the poor fellow in the next aisle got a frightful going over — he did have a lot of written material. Every magazine and book had to be carefully checked for seditious material.

One last customs story: We arrived in Seattle after six weeks in the Far East. For us it was just a refuelling stop on the way to Dublin. But a big amazon of a customs lady didn't see it that way. Every packet had to be opened and every dirty underpants displayed for her attention.

As we tried to get them all back again she turned to Peter Canning and asked him where he was going.

"We are on our way back to Ireland," he said with as much civility as he could muster.

"Oh, you're going to Ireland, are you? My name is Irish. Maybe you've heard of it? McQuaid!"

Pssst. Guess who!

15

The Clerical Club

We were staying in the bishop's house in Antigua, West Indies so it was easy to find a clerical directory. I looked up the name and telephone number of the priest in Dominica in whose parish we wished to film and phoned him.

"I am a priest from Dublin, Ireland," I said, "and I want to film in your parish. Can you collect me at the airport? Put up a technician and myself for one or two nights? And give us the use of your car for two days?

Great! And eh, oh yes, — the use of your car.

"Come," he said. And we came.

He turned out to be French.

Some years later there was a hurricane in Dominica and enormous damage was done in his area. It was so bad that a photograph and story appeared in an Irish newspaper. Soon after I had a letter from the same parish priest. It was his turn to be in need. I sent $400.

We went to Mexico recently. The Irish Missionary Union told me that the Divine Word Missionaries had a house in the capital. I phoned three days before leaving and booked in a party of four, indefinitely. We were met at Mexico airport at 12 midnight and brought to our quarters.

By virtue of trade, profession or hobby most people belong to a loose international club; sailors are welcome in any yacht club in the world, lawyers in courts, and doctors in foreign hospitals. But the clerical club international, I suggest, offers better facilities for film makers than any other. We can send a crew almost anywhere in the world and arrange accommodation at a moment's notice. Once installed we can come and go as we will, raid the fridge, borrow the landrover or car, telephone home, and walk out without paying for a sausage. (Mind you we do give an offering, but nobody ever asks for it.) Religious houses are also very valuable centres of information as to who's who, who knows what, where to go, and how to get things done.

Of course they vary in service and quality. American houses are the most comfortable — sylvan settings, well stocked fridges and private swimming pools. Third world seminaries on the other hand may mean four to a room, no running water and black beans for breakfast, dinner and tea.

I could tell hundreds of stories where the clerical club has smoothed our path in film making. The most recent one comes from a trip in 1986 to Mexico.

There were notices in the hotels in San Cristobal de las Casas, Chiapas, South Mexico, that photography is not permitted in certain towns in the surrounding region during fiestas. One of these is Tenejapa.

One of the problems film makers have in third world countries is that people often prefer not to have their photographs taken by wealthy tourists. And who can blame them! Sometimes it is because they feel they are being treated like animals in a zoo, or sometimes because they feel people will make money out of their image, or in the case of tribal people, because they believe that every time a photo is taken, they lose part of their soul. An interesting notion – not too stupid when you think about it. This view is far more widespread than I would ever have believed and because of it, I've had oranges thrown at me in Mexico, dirt in the New Territories, Hong Kong, and water in the Philippines. Whatever their reasons, and we did not ask, the people of Tenajapa will not let anyone photograph their fiesta without the express permission of the village president.

But the fiesta sounded interesting and we were anxious to include it in a film about the church and the indigenous people who lived near San Cristobal.

The local priest was new and didn't know his way around. But two religious sisters kept a little paper shop in town to help pay the bills. They were natives of the town and one of them promised to arrange to get permission from the president.

But when we arrived on the morning of the fiesta and went with her to see the president, he was away up the hills. So we started talking to his deputy and members of the council trying to explain our mission. At that moment a big station wagon arrived and we were joined by another European and his lovely daughter, or secretary, or something. Peter Lemass was making heavy weather explaining that viewers in Ireland would be very interested to see something of Mexican culture and that if a film crew came over to Ireland from Tenejapa they would of course be given every facility . . . (all this had to be said in Spanish and translated piecemeal into Tzotzel, the local language). He went on further to explain how we in Ireland were also once oppressed and exploited and understood what it meant to be a people struggling to keep their own culture in face of outside pressures and

96

competition . . .

"Nonsense," said the European speaking for the first time in an Oxford accent, "there's no parallel whatever." And then he gave us a little lecture.

"I've been around these parts some twenty-seven years. And you come around and expect to arrange to film the same day! You have to let the people get to know you and live for some time around the place before you can expect to be accepted."

We ignored him. The nun explained to the Council that we were not ordinary tourists but padres.

At this stage the Englishman's patience came to an end. "Would you mind letting me get along with my business please," he said.

"Go ahead," said Peter, "We're not stopping you."

So he proceeded to tell the elders of the village that he had got permission some days ago from the president to film.

"Have you got the permission in writing?" asked the nun.

"No. It was given verbally."

"Well, it has to be written. No permission is valid unless written."

There was a long pause. The second in command suggested that the Englishman go off and find the president up the hills, over one hour's journey by landrover over dreadful roads.

After much agonising, a frustrated film-maker left for the mountains to look for the president.

As soon as they had gone, one of the elders suggested to the nun that if she had a word with the cow and told him we were padres, it might be possible to come to some arrangement. (The cow was a key performer at the fiesta.)

In the end it cost us $7 to film away to our hearts' content. This was a very cheap rate. One tourist was asked $10 for a single still photo.

Then when we'd finished one hour later, the rain came down. And I am afraid we laughed and laughed all the way home at the thought of one very irate English director, slipping and sliding over wet rocky roads, looking for the president's written permission.

16

Issues and Impressions

Over the past twenty-five years Radharc has made two hundred and fifty films in fifty-nine different countries. I have personally directed films in forty-nine of them. Coming to a country to make films for television is quite different from coming as a tourist. One is under severe pressure to try and understand what is going on in the social, political and especially the religious fields.

And since no film is made by one person but by a group, there is a constant debate going on over the whole production period. Every interview is typed out and pored over and cut and recut until parts of it enter one's permanent memory.

Based on this experience, the following are some impressions and reflections, the latter relating to some of the great issues now facing the Catholic Church.

The Irish Empire
One abiding impression is that the Catholic Church in the territories which once formed part of the British Empire is largely an Irish creation.

In Australia, New Zealand and the Pacific islands, there were thirty-one bishops in 1892. Twenty-one of them were Irish born.

Between 1800 and 1900, seventy-five per cent of all the priests who worked in Australia were Irish born. As late as 1960, half the priests in the diocese of Florida were Irish born. Many of the rest had Irish names. Los Angeles had a Irish-speaking Archbishop up to last year. His successor is called Mahony.

I stayed two years ago in a parish in Grenada in the West Indies.

Most of the parish priests in the last century were Irish, and some even in the previous century; and being all secular priests they must have come to Grenada by their own choice.

In much of English speaking Africa and especially in Nigeria, Sierra Leone, Tanzania and Kenya, the Catholic Church is largely the creation of Irish missionaries. A Nigerian bishop said of Bishop Shanahan from Tipperary, "He was our St Patrick".

And it wasn't only the priests!

We stayed in a presbytery in Bridgetown, Barbados. The church was called St Patrick's. When I made the customary offering at the end of our stay, the parish priest, a native Bajian, refused to take any money.

"How could I?" He said, "When your countrymen built this place."

And for the first time in struck me why churches called after St Patrick spring up in the oddest places — Bangalore in India and Iscamabad in Pakistan are other unusual examples.

In every garrison town in the British Empire there would always be a substantial contingent of troops who were Irish and Catholic. They built their own churches and called them after St Patrick!

Astronaut to mission control: "Request check out of Irish space programme."

Women in the Church
I think the most significant changes in the church of the future may well come from the efforts of women to claim some share in the exercise of authority. The movement towards change is most apparent in North America. "Who'd want to be a man trying to explain American women to Roman men?" wailed one American bishop.

But the unease is by no means confined to the US. Archbishop, (now Cardinal) Daneels of Malines said to us in an interview in 1978:

"I think many young women and young mothers are leaving the church very silently — this could be the most dangerous haemorrhage in the history of the church. And perhaps one of the symptoms of that is the absence of religious vocations among young people, especially women."

Women's place is in the cave.
That's what I say!

I once wrote in *The Furrow* that "the only way that second class citizens in the Church can become less second class (this group includes brothers and nuns as well as laity) is by achieving an intellectual eminence in theological fields. When a future Vatican Council takes place (be it the third or the tenth), where most bishops are accompanied by lay theologians, then and only then will there manifestly be lay participation in the area of Church life where it really matters."

This is already happening in a way with American women. Sixty-five per cent of sisters in America have a master's degree or better, compared with twenty-four per cent of the bishops. Twenty-five per cent of religious sisters have doctorates, compared with ten per cent of bishops.

Yet the situation remains where a priest or deacon without even a BA to his name will automatically be licensed to preach in church, whereas a woman with a double doctorate in theology is forbidden to speak.

That situation will be hard to maintain.

100

In the church of Rome, where tradition plays such an important part, women theologians look for models in the past — in other words, where have women been able to exercise authority in the Church; where have they been taken seriously; where have men and women worked together in equality and harmony to further the kingdom of God?

Where indeed but in Ireland and in areas of mainland Britain where the Irish evangelised! Ita, Ebba, Hilda, Moninne of Killeavy, and above all Brigid were not religious women in our present understanding of that term. They exercised authority of a quasi-episcopal nature. And so they are of special interest today, and the object of special study.

Margaret MacCurtain, a Dominican nun and historian from University College Dublin, spoke about Brigid for a programme on the celtic monasteries:

"St Brigid, of course, is the leading example we have, even to the present time, of what leadership in the early church for women meant, because not only did she found a monastery, a healing city for men and women, both celibates and lay people, but she also, as far as we can make out, exercised the jurisdiction of a bishop. This practice was continued by her successors for several centuries after her death.

A persistent legend got into the Annals from about the 8th century onwards that her great friend, St Mel of Longford, a bishop, was invited to install her as abbess in her monastery in Kildare. The story goes that he read over her the office of a bishop, i.e. the consecration of a bishop, and the legend concludes with the words 'and thereafter Brigid and her successors ruled as bishops of Kildare.'

There is, in fact, substantial truth in this, and evidence as well, because both Brigid and her successors as abbesses did appoint the local bishop and the priests and exercised the jurisdiction of a bishop. And this was not unusual, according to the historian Fr. John Ryan."

There is no suggestion of course that Brigid or any other woman exercised the function of Orders. Brigid worked with a bishop — Conleth by name.

"Some sources of course think that Conleth was a kind of pet or retainer bishop whom she appointed. Now this is quite unfair to Conleth. He actually represents the kind of male-female complementarity that can be found in the early church, where the leader of the local church happens to be a woman and where the kind of male counterpart is not an accommodating male who does what she tells him. Instead, Conleth fits in easily and is at home in that kind of setting. I would say Conleth was a man who was very much at ease with his own sexuality and quite happy to be an organiser in an important city abbey, the double abbey of Kildare. The kind of authority that he exercised was undoubtedly that of a bishop, but there is no doubt about it that he derived in some way his jurisdiction from Brigid as abbess."

World Population
One has to live a while in Asia to have any right to talk about over-population.

It's not just that the towns and cities are crowded — of course they are, but that can be true in any country. I think it's a feeling that first struck me in South India — the *countryside* as well as the towns is crawling with people. A priest in Korea put it to me crudely — there's virtually no place you could go in the country and have a crap behind a bush or tree and not expect to have an audience.

Inchon is the main port for the capital of Korea, Seoul. Outside the railway station there is a digital clock which shows the population of the country in figures visible at half a mile. There are seventeen such clocks planned for all the major cities, all connected to a central computer which monitors the increase in population. As we watched it seemed to register one additional person each minute.

The population of Korea has doubled in the past twenty-five

years — from twenty million to forty million. The clocks are part of a government programme to persuade people to have less children. One is the ideal; two is permitted. After two the State bears down and begins to make life difficult.

The clear impression one gets in any third world country, and especially in Asia, is that despite *Humanae Vitae,* the contraception problem is by no means resolved for Catholic Christians.

One finds different attitudes among Bishops. The last remaining Irish bishop in Korea for example is a strong promoter of natural family planning.

Many admire his single mindedness and enthusiasm. Many non-Catholic Koreans are attracted to the method because it is in tune with nature; because it avoids the side effects of other contraceptives, and because it is more effective than most people seem to believe.

Be that as it may, the Bishop's enthusiasm is not obviously shared by his Korean episcopal brethren who give lip service to natural methods, but put little effort or resources into publicising them.

The problem is that the method requires periodic abstinence, a certain sophistication among those who use it, and a high degree of motivation. Clearly the Bishops don't feel the average Korean couple is capable of all three.

Other hierarchies have taken a tougher approach.

In 1980 the Archbishop of Jakarta said to us: "So the Catholics of Indonesia are supposed to do the family planning through abstinence but in the reality now and then we get some problems. Take this: if there are husband and wife who are really not able to have another child, but on the other hand, they are really not able to use the abstinence to prevent the birth of the new child, so, I think we cannot ask the impossible. What is impossible we cannot ask from people, and therefore the bishops of Indonesia have said, in this situation, I mean in this predicament, people are allowed to use other means provided it is not abortion and not sterilisation.

Q. What was the feeling in Rome about the Indonesian bishops' stand?

A. Of course, there was a reaction. The first reaction was from Rome.

Q. How did they react?

A. We have answered Rome and we have — we are explaining what we mean by this, that we as bishops, we have also a pastoral problem. Our saying is stiff in front of the people and there are many poor people who are really not able to practise natural family planning. That's our problem and we have to help these people too. We cannot say to them that they are sinning every day, that they are sinners. But we have to help them and I think we are trying to do both, namely – we are trying to promote the natural family planning but we are trying also to give a pastoral solution in the meantime.

Dr Riberi, spokesman for the Indonesian bishops added:

You can say the Vatican would like that we change our stand in this matter you know. But we think as a particular church we have also the right to have our own policy regarding the implementation of universal laws you know. And we think that the Indonesian situation is so urgent that we are not quite responsible when we don't think seriously about a way out to face up to our population problems.

And what is the attitude of Irish missionaries?

I tried to probe this once. It was clear first of all that many of them would prefer not to be asked about it. But I met nobody who was prepared to tell every couple using artificial contraception that they were committing serious sin.

A common answer was, "I don't have problems any more about that." But in this case it often seemed to me than they had decided not to have any more problems, without actually resolving the issue in their own minds.

Another common approach was expressed by one priest as follows:

I don't see any contradiction in putting forward an ideal, but then I feel at the same time that if we are to stand by the Church's teaching on the rights of the couple's conscience, then it's not up to me as a priest to decide for them.

This seems to me a rather dubious position. A priest wouldn't say to somebody, the Church teaches that murder is wrong, but if you feel you can't live up to this ideal, and need to kill somebody, make up your own mind.

Other missionaries simply reject the teaching. This may be a muted rejection — I don't have problems. Or it may be straight from the shoulder. A professor of moral theology in a seminary once said to me, "the pope made a mistake, and we have to live with it until one of his successors alters the teaching, or lets it fall into abeyance."

While there is diversity of view of how to meet the problems raised by *Humanae Vitae*, there would be general agreement on all sides that the Church's credibility as a teaching organisation is very much weakened by the wide range of attitudes among bishops and priests, ranging from compliance, to lack of enthusiasm, to outright rejection.

The teaching church has three options: change the teaching, or let it be quietly forgotten, or enforce it. The present policy is as far as possible to enforce it. The Archbishop of Jakarta, quoted above, told us that the Indonesian bishops were under severe pressure to come to Rome and get brainwashed (his term).

It would be hard to prove, but it is said that no man nowadays will be appointed a bishop unless he indicates total acceptance of *Humanae Vitae*.

I know of one case where this prevented a man being a bishop. Archbishop Dermot Ryan called me round to his house one day — a rather unusual event. The main purpose was to tell me that he was thinking of asking for X as an auxiliary bishop, and wanted my opinion. I said I thought it would be a good idea, and gave my reasons even though it was quite clear to me he had made up his mind already, and was only looking for confirmation. Some months after, I met Dermot in quite a public place. He obviously had something agitating him. He pulled me into a corner and said, "There's somebody trying to spike X. I don't know who it is,

105

but I'm going to find out." I never heard who was trying to spike him, but I heard the reason. It was reported to Rome that he had said or written something critical of *Humanae Vitae*. I never knew that he had, but he never became a bishop.

A policy of excluding anybody from the episcopacy who may at some time have expressed reservations about *Humanae Vitae*, while understandable, could have other long-term effects. There are clearly greater chances of promotion for the sycophant, the ambitious, the safe-sider and those who are just dull. The brighter minds, who tend often to be questioning minds, may not be careful enough to avoid at some time saying something which would fail them in this litmus test.

There was one other incident in our travels which I felt at the time was a significant indicator:

Fr Tom Stack and I were filming in Rome during the 1980 Synod on the family. At supper one evening, an Irish bishop attending the Synod remarked on an interesting contribution by Archbishop Hurley of Durban.

Hurley had put forward what he at least felt were some new theological insights which might permit fresh thinking on the contraceptive issue.

We looked in the Osservatore next day, but there was no mention in the report on the Synod of any intervention by Archbishop Hurley. So we went to the Vatican Press Office and asked for a copy of his speech. There was no record of any speech by Hurley. So we got in touch with the Archbishop. He only had some notes because he had passed on his text to the Press Office so they would be sure to get it right.

That's what is called news management.

Abortion

There are fashions in religion as in everything else. The big growth area in Buddhism in Japan are temples in honour of a god called the bodhisattva Jizo. We filmed in a temple to Jizo near Kamakuru, Japan. There were images of Jizo, and thousands upon thousands of statue dolls dressed in child's clothing and surrounded by the kinds of things that children love — toys, chewing gum and plastic coloured wheels that turn in the wind.

Visitors to the temple offered alms, incense, lit a taper at their own particular statue doll, left more gifts and openly prayed.

It seems the Japanese have two methods of handling the guilt caused by abortions. One way is to try and discipline the mind

106

to dismiss feelings of guilt as irrational. The other is to conduct what are called mizuyo kuyu services in honour of Jizo.

The doll represents the aborted baby. The toys are gifts for him or her to play with. Revealing messages are left lying around.

"I aborted my first baby. I want my second child to be free from any bad feelings that the first child might have . . ."

"My baby. I am sorry. You came too early for us." "I came here to apologise. I feel guilty. Please forgive your foolish father."

In Buddhist teaching, life begins at conception. And while abortion is tolerated in Japan, the growth of the Jizo cult shows that there is a natural revulsion to it which cannot so easily be swept away.

Opposition to abortion is also one of the most deeply held convictions in the Catholic tradition.

A Korean catholic surgeon, who was also leader of the prayer group in his parish, told us for instance that he had no problems about contraception or sterilisation, but that he refused to perform abortions.

The vast majority of missionaries fully support traditional church teaching on abortion, though many would feel that the church is in a weaker position when it couples opposition to abortion with opposition to artificial contraception. Again some point to the experience of Japan. Despite Buddhist aversion to abortion, Japan has the highest abortion rate in Asia, if not in the world. Japan is also one of the few countries in the world which bans the contraceptive pill — a fact which often comes as a surprise to Westerners. This prohibition is said to have come about because of the harmful side effects of the pill. Its critics say that the real reason is that the decision was made by men who were anxious to maintain the traditional Japanese control over their womenfolk, and deny them any say in when they may or may not bear children. No doubt the ban will be removed, and probably soon. It will be interesting to see what effect, if any, that may have on the rate of abortions.

Human Life is Sacred
Barbara Donaghy and her friends made 35,000 clay models of American nuclear armaments, including missiles and submarines. They spread them out in rows in a large open space in Washington – acres of them. They called their effort a "Miniature US Atomic Arsenal".

It took something graphic like that to bring home to me the obscenity of the arms race. 35,000 warheads are enough to explode one atomic bomb every day of the year for 96 years! Not little primitive bombs like those used at Hiroshima or Nagasaki, but medium sized ones capable of killing a million people each.

It was a kind of conversion. Before that I looked on Bruce Kent, the Greenham Commons ladies and peace people generally with a benign, but slightly amused and patronising air. I am beginning to think now that they are the only people who are really sane. When a naval officer in charge of a submarine is put in a position where he may have to decide to release twenty missiles, each carrying eight warheads, each warhead capable of destroying a city of one million people, then all other questions of human life — abortion, contraception, over population — become relatively less significant. The problem in our time is the survival of humanity.

From time to time the Pope, the Vatican office, bishops' conferences, individual bishops make statements about peace which are worthy and true. There is a World Day of Peace and the Holy Father or some of his minions write a message. It's all very predictable and predictably it has little effect. But there have been cases where a few bishops have really stuck their neck out in the peace issue; two examples we came across in America were Archbishop Hunthausen and Bishop Sullivan. It's odd, and maybe accidental, but they are also the only two bishops in the US who have been publicly investigated by the Vatican in recent times — ostensibly on other issues. Hunthausen was so shaken that he got a heart attack immediately after the investigation.

The Church of the rich and the Church of the poor
The better part of Santiago de Chile is on the side of the hills. This is where the wealthy and the middle class live. Down below in the valley are the shanty towns and slums.

The people who live on the sides of the hills are all served by Chilean priests, but no Chilean clergy work in the valley. Foreign missionaries serve the people in the slums.

Sometimes the Chilean priests betray their embarrassment to the foreigner:

"You seem to understand these people far better than we do. We wouldn't know how to talk to them."

When I asked Archbishop Romero about the very different attitudes of Latin American bishops with regard to the so-called option for the poor, he replied:

"The documents of Pueblo deal with this explicitly. They say that in Latin America not all of us have yet been converted to the poor. It's important to underline that. Because when one is not converted to the poor one looks everywhere for other explanations.

But the message of Pueblo to the people of Latin America tells us that the option for the poor isn't for some and not for others. It calls on all social classes to interest themselves in the poor as though it were their own cause. As though it were, as indeed it always has been, the cause of Christ who said, 'what you do to one of my brothers, you do to me.'

I think it's very simple. We should take an interest in the suffering of the poor as though it was happening to us."

One of the misconceptions, which perhaps people in broadcasting and the press help to perpetuate, is that people like Archbishop Romero are somehow typical of the Latin American Church.

Monsignor Romero did embrace the option for the poor. But in this he was alone and exceptional among the bishops of El Salvador. And he died for it.

It's quite difficult to convey the difference between a Romero and the other bishops in El Salvador. But I'll try.

Ten priests wrote to the newspapers in El Salvador saying that they were tired of seeing pictures of the Papal Nuncio at this or that cocktail party or diplomatic reception, and hoped in future they might see his picture visiting one of the poorer barrios.

Their bishop suspended them from saying public Mass for six months, which also meant they received no salary.

The views of Bishop Aparicio of San Vicente in El Salvador as expressed to me in October 1979 are fairly representative of a typical Latin American bishop:

"Archbishop Romero, mainly because of his views, or perhaps as a result of his inexperience, was manipulated by a group of young diocesan priests, and in a very special way by the Jesuits. Then these priests began to give the pastoral work of the church a political orientation. They were talking about taking political power, and they used the Bible Study Groups to prepare the ground for their future activities. From that time on, there was the division between the pastoral orientation of the archdiocese (of San Salvador) and the other dioceses.

The pastoral orientation of the archdiocese is too politicised and they have used the peasants to preach a pastoral full of hate for the rich and the military.

Several times we (the other bishops) have suggested to Archbishop Romero that we should talk together personally on a one to one basis, without him always having a team of Jesuits and others behind him. We should just stand as a church in front of God to resolve our problems.

I feel we can have hope in the young military men and in the present government. I said that clearly to the Minister of Defence, to whom I'm now preparing to send my last sermon. So far, he has been an honourable person, and when he was in charge of the armed forces in San Vicente he was able to work with all classes of society. And that is why we have hope.''

A very good sermon, Bishop. I particularly like the bit about not knowing the day nor the hour.

Romero was summoned to Rome several times to give an account of himself. He found little sympathy there. They had a file as long as your arm of complaints from other bishops.

Without support at home or in Rome, he must have understood that his days were numbered. The man who shot him in the heart

110

during the consecration of the Mass must also have known how much he stood alone.

Only one member of the Hierarchy of El Salvador found time to attend his funeral.

Nobody came from Rome to pick up the chalice that fell from his hands. Indeed the Vatican allowed his murder to pass almost uncommented on. The chief mourners at his funeral were the poor.

I was fortunate once to be present at an all day meeting of clergy and sisters working in the diocese of El Salvador, which Romero himself attended.

Watching and photographing the faces of the people around him, it was clear that for many of them even then, he was a source of inspiration and hope.

Now that seems even more true in death.

In those parts of the Church that like to think of themselves as the church of the poor, his portrait is on every wall and his picture in every prayer book.

Earlier this year (1986) we talked to a bishop in Mexico who had spent all his life with the impoverished Indian people. "I have no degree, my degrees are the Indians on the mountains," is the way he described himself.

He tries to take seriously the "option for the poor", which meant, as seems usual nowadays, he was denounced to the Vatican as a dangerous marxist.

The Apostolic Delegate put pressure on him to go to Rome. He tried to opt out saying that he hadn't the fare. But the fare was supplied by the Delegate, and he had to go.

He described his visit with much humour. How he had to borrow the correct clothes, how when the Swiss Guard said "Eccellenza" and clicked his heels, he looked around to see what important person was coming behind him!

Eventually he came to present his report to the Pope, and here I let him tell the story.

He, (the Pope) was thumbing through the report, reading and listening to me telling how the diocese is divided, distribution of priests, sisters, mission houses, the pastoral work beginning with diocesan objectives, pastoral priorities, the hope of the Kingdom being realised . . . when he said:

"Your work is not marxist".

(I thought to myself, it was worthwhile coming to Rome!) And I asked him:

111

"What did you say, Your Holiness?
"That your work is not communist, it's not marxist. Continue right on . . ."
Well I was so happy and grateful . . ."

When one considers the recent history of Poland, one can understand why the present Pope would have very strong reservations about communism and marxism. And if communism always has to be of the imperialistic Russian type, I for one would agree with him.

But political theories can be what you make of them. I see no essential reason why communism need be imperialistic or atheistic. I think that because of short-sighted American policies, and cold war attitudes, countries like Cuba which would like to be socialist, are thrown into the Russian camp because no one else is willing to give them the market they need to survive.

There is one central problem in Central America, the grossly unfair distribution of wealth. Much of which is rooted in the injustices of the Spanish conquest.

Not all of us have been converted to the poor.

In Guatemala, 5% of the population share 60% of the national earnings. At the other end of the scale, 50% of the population share 7% of the income.

In El Salvador, 8% of the population own 90% of the arable land. Or put it another way, 92% of the population share 10% of the arable land. Clearly this is grossly unjust, and cannot be in accordance with the will of God.

There has to be a levelling down and a redistribution of resources before there can ever be peace. No elected parliamentary democracy in the present situation could possibly achieve this: the vested interests are too great.

If there has to be a levelling down, a left wing government is the only type that could conceivably achieve it.

112

Latin America is very different from Eastern Europe. It is a lot further from Russia for one thing. The people are different too. A socialist Chile will no more want to be part of the Soviet Block than China or Vietnam.

When the great discrepancies of wealth have been evened out, and society has settled down again, then men and women will begin again to think of the need for greater freedom. That is the way they are made.

The sad thing about this scenario is that the United States will do its utmost to prevent it happening. And the reason is not really that anyone in the US cares whether Brazilians or Chileans call themselves communists.

The lesson of Cuba for the US is that when a Caribbean or Latin American state becomes firmly left wing, all the professional and wealthy classes leave and descend on the United States. The rich have to lose money and position if the poor are to become richer, and the rich don't like losing. One million left Cuba for the US.

If Central America, including Mexico, were to get left wing governments, more millions of hispanic Americans would descend on California, Texas and Florida.

Understandably the US government is trying to avoid this situation. In the meantime however, the cost for Central and South American countries in suffering, death and destruction is so great that it is probably beyond the comprehension of anybody who hasn't spent some time there.

Liberation Theology et al.
One of my ambitions in life is to take time off to read and think about the problem of violence. Is it ever permitted in the Christian context? Or must one always turn the other cheek?

The use of the word "violence" of course prejudges the issue. Because violence can only be defined as the unjust use of force. But is there ever a *just* use of force?

Pope John Paul II has been single minded in his condemnation of the use of physical force in any form. His would appear to be the truly Christian attitude. Christ could have called down legions of angels to destroy his enemies, but he didn't. On the other hand I don't think the problem is that simple.

Christ drove out the money changers with whips which seems a violent thing to do. And scattered all their money and possessions.

Who could condemn the people of Nicaragua for trying to oust the Samoza family by force? Ruthless exploiters who cornered for

113

themselves most of the wealth of Nicaragua and tortured and shot anyone who opposed them.

I once sat with a group of peasant women studying the scriptures in El Salvador. The text which one of them read and all discussed was "The Vineyard of Naboth" from the Book of Kings.

For those whose knowledge of the Old Testament may have grown a little faint, the story runs briefly as follows:

Naboth had a vineyard close to the Palace of King Ahab, King of Samaria. Ahab wanted the vineyard as a vegetable garden; it could come in handy because it adjoined his own property. He offered to buy it, but Naboth was unwilling to sell because it had belonged to his family for many generations. Ahab was annoyed, and sulked, refusing to eat. When his wife Jezebel enquired the reason he told her the story. She replied:

> "You make a fine King of Israel, and no mistake! Get up and eat; cheer up and you will feel better; I will get you the vineyard of Naboth of Jezreel myself . . ."

So she arranged to have Naboth murdered. Ahab didn't ask any questions, but was happy enough to take the land.

> Then the word of Yahweh came to Elijah, the Tishbite. Up! Go down and meet Ahab king of Israel in Samaria. You will find him in Naboth's vineyard; he has gone down to take possession of it.
>
> You are to say this to him. Yahweh says this: 'You have committed murder; now you usurp as well. For this — and Yahweh says this — in the place where the dogs licked the blood of Naboth, the dogs will lick your blood too.'

In a country where 90% of the arable land is owned by 8% of the people, that is heady material. In a country where the peasantry are squeezed like oranges — I borrow the image from a Salvadorean peasant — where men pick coffee for fourteen hours and earn two or three dollars, who dares to say, "suffer and be quiet"?

In terms of the Third World, it seems to me that the most significant change in the Church since the first preaching of Christianity is the re-presentation of the message in modern terms as a gospel of liberation, a gospel which emphasises the words of Jesus when he unrolled the scroll of the Bible before a hushed audience in the synagogue and used the words of Isaiah to sum up his mission:

The Lord has sent me to bring good news to the poor:
To proclaim liberty to captives,
And the blind new sight.
To set the downtrodden free.

I concluded the El Salvador film with the following script, which I would still stand over, though it may now seem a bit pretentious:

The commitment of the Church to the poor, and the belief now so widely held that the Gospel can only be fairly presented in Latin America as a gospel of liberation, can only mean that dragons' teeth of one kind or another are being sown.

So there *will* be change. How soon and how bloody depends on the determination of the rich, backed by the military, to postpone it.

The army provided a firework display for the fiesta in Gotera. The legends reads: "Long live the armed forces commandos." One can join with that. May they live long, by not shooting or getting shot by their fellow countrymen; who would also like to live long — without poverty, or disease, or assassination, or torture, or being deprived of the dignity which is their right as free and responsible human beings.

The struggle is proving to be long and bloody, and perhaps bloodier than a lot of enthusiasts for liberation might have expected. Some are quite shaken and confused.

I sensed this very strongly among church people in Guatemala in 1984. The attrition there had been frightful. Thirty priests and religious, and hundreds of highly trained delegates of the Word — lay people qualified to take over some of the work formerly done by priests — had been killed. One million people routed out of their homes. Two hundred thousand fled to surrounding countries. Eight thousand killed in a year.

A quiet American Benedictine who had lived some time in Guatemala spoke to me of his attempts to discuss the awful situation with army people:

"This army fellow was one of the men out in the field that had to direct the units that do what they call 'a clean-up'. And he said that one of the basic rules that they use is that if they found there was a band of armed men in a country area, and especially if they had machine-guns and heavy equipment, that they would simply decide that anybody in that area, men, women, children,

115

would be wiped out, because they would all in some way or other be involved in helping the guerrilla movement. And so they would simply kill everybody. For example, the kids, the reason why they wouldn't want them around is because they would be able to tell other people what had happened, and who was there, and all kinds of other things. In other words they'd be witnesses – which they wouldn't want. The women would be involved in making food and feeding the guerrillas, so they'd be guilty. And so, since it's just impossible to decide that this person, that person would not be guilty, they would just simply wipe out everybody. And from a military point of view, you can see that such a simplistic attitude is very easy to follow and you can tell your men what to do and very easily they can do it. But from the viewpoint of justice and human rights, of course, it's terrible.

An Irish Sister working in Guatemala – whom I would prefer not to identify — added the following:

The effects of the killings was the insecurity of who would be killed next. People said to me, "we leave our home, and we don't know what will happen when we are away." Also some of those people were taken off buses, and so they fear even to come to market and sell the things they need to sell to make money to buy clothes or keep the children at school. They fear to do that because maybe in the process they will get killed. I think the fear of even having children – people with a culture that appreciate children saying, "why should we have children now because if we have children, especially boys, maybe they are just going to be killed in the future, and that's going to be suffering for us?" So there was a change in their own culture pattern from a rural trusting people to a people who felt that for no reason they could be killed.

The violence of the backlash by the rich, and by the army which they control, has appalled many missionaries in Central America. The whole situation has been made much worse by the very conservative nature of the present US government under Ronald Reagan which has thrown the resources of the United States government on the side of opposition to change.

There is no question that there has been a certain drawing back by the Church in Guatemala. A certain de-emphasis of liberation theology and a certain confusion as to what to substitute. I don't think this is because the Vatican is unhappy with some of the liberation theologians. Nor can I see the reverse as permanent.

It is inconceivable that the Church could return to accepting the situation summed up in the hymn, "The rich man in his castle, and the poor man at his gate. God made them high or lowly, and ordered their estate."

But the people of Guatemala have been terribly hurt by the army and the rich. There must at least be a respite in their drawn out struggle for justice. To quote the Irish sister again:

> Because we see people suffering, maybe suffering more deeply than we've seen before, one becomes more reflective in the struggle for justice. One reflects, would it be better leave them suffering to avoid their being killed . . . so I think now the priests and the pastoral agents are trying to continue in the search for justice, but at the same time maybe being more careful about how that's expressed. The continual struggle for justice is being made more difficult by the influx of sectarian groups who just say, "if you praise Jesus Christ, maybe you don't have to look at the social condition, and so it could be a temptation to us too to say let's praise Jesus Christ, and forget about the social condition of our brothers and sisters." But this would not be progress on the road to justice, and to a true christianisation of our situation.

Driving around Tonga, in the South Pacific, one cannot help being struck by the number of villages that have very large, well equipped and new Mormon churches.

The churches have schools attached and anyone who does well at school gets a free scholarship to a Mormon university in the United States.

Now whereas most people in the US dream of getting away to a tropical island, most people on tropical islands dream of going to the US. So there can be natural attractions to joining the Mormons and many people do. Which leaves the traditional churches, including the Catholic Church, unamused.

The Mormons have two advantages which make them hard to beat, even though their theology seems weird to us. First of all every Mormon is expected to give 10% of his income to his church. That's a lot of bread. Every Mormon is expected to give two years of his life to mission work. That's a lot of dedication.

The Mormons are also very active in Central and South America along with other fundamentalist groups originating in the US.

117

Now right-wing American governments, North, Central and South, don't like liberation theology which they call "the theology of subversion". So they are not too adverse to the Mormons or other fundamentalist groups coming in and providing a little competition for the Catholic Church. Make them run scared and perhaps they may become less enthusiastic for liberation! Undoubtedly this has had an effect, particularly on the more conservative clergy, who feel that the Church's interests are being endangered by too much talk about issues of justice and peace.

The Mexican bishops have spoken out recently on this issue and implied the backing of the CIA for fundamentalist groups.

Central and South America are particularly vulnerable to fundamentalist penetration. In the past the Hierarchies in the former Spanish dominions were appointed by the Spanish King. All or almost all the lower clergy came from Spain. As a matter of policy no indigenous Americans were ordained. The Kings of Spain wanted it that way because they realised that a local clergy might well foment rebellion. Safer to keep the Church in Spanish hands. Spain had too many clerics anyway; export markets were needed to relieve the pressure at home!

Even today, the Church in Latin America depends heavily on foreign — mostly Spanish — clergy. They have no tradition of supplying their own priests.

Now the Catholic Church has always been a very clerical church. Priests do things or they are not done at all. Today at least this has begun to change in an attempt to meet the challenge posed by the Mormons and other right wing sects.

Take Putre for instance. There hasn't been a resident priest in this small Chilean town for fifty years. Nowadays a priest from Arica comes up once a month, if he is able. But the Mormon elders were born in Putre and live there all the time. So they have cleaned up.

The Church has responded to the challenge by promoting Basic Ecclesial Communities. They used to be called Basic *Christian* Communities, but the bishops were afraid of them in the beginning because they were felt to be an attempt to form an alternative church outside the institutional clerical framework. Now that it is realised that they can be a valuable tool to fight the fundamentalists, they have been accepted and legitimised by substituting 'ecclesial' (ie. church) for "Christian".

Basic Communities usually start with a group studying and reflecting on the Bible, using the 'See, Judge, Act' method. In

118

this way Christians become accustomed to looking at the world through the eyes of the Gospel and to committing themselves to action which may make it a more Christian place.

So Basic Communities become action communities within the Church and the wider society. Members may get involved as individuals in religious instruction or go further and accept longterm training as Delegates of the Word – sort of lay priests.

Delegates provide everything a native priesthood might provide – except they can't say Mass or hear Confession. This development is extremely significant and provides quite a new model for the Roman Church.

In Kiribati, formerly the Gilbert Islands, the bishop has the largest (in area) diocese in the world. And about nine active priests.

If you call to the presbytery up the road from the Cathedral, you'll find a married man, his wife and four children living there and holding the church keys. He does baptisms and marriages and preaches and conducts a communion service that is almost a Mass. He is a quasi priest, who if permission ever came through from Rome, could be ordained the next day. In the meantime, he and about three hundred others run a vibrant church and try to make maximum use of their few celibate priests.

17

The rationale of priests working in broadcasting

Not so many years ago, when I was looking for a priest of the Dublin diocese to work for me, I wrote a short memorandum pointing out that if every one of the six hundred priests working in parishes in the diocese were to deliver two sermons each Sunday for seven minutes to a congregation of approximately four hundred people, it would take two years to achieve the same exposure to audience as a year's Radharc programmes on RTÉ.

Of course, qualifications can be made on both sides.

Many viewers may not be watching television even though their set is on. Yes, and the people in the pews may be sleeping through the sermon. The television programme may have nothing of religious importance to say: The preacher may have nothing of religious importance to say. The programme could be made by laymen: The sermon could be preached by laymen. And so on.

I offer Mass every morning like the other priests with whom I was ordained. After Mass they may work at a variety of jobs. As manager of the local school they may have to do something about the heating system which has just broken down. Or sit in on the selection of a new teacher. Having responsibility for the church fabric means they may have to chase the roofing contractor who was supposed to come last week to mend the leak in the sacristy. If it's a Monday they'll have to count the money from the previous day's collection. If there's a choir, perhaps they need a choir practice. Then there's the parish draw and the door to door collection. And all the Easter Dues envelopes which have to be checked and acknowledged. There is the delegation to be met who wish to use the parish hall for adult education classes. All of these things could be done, and perhaps better done, by laymen.

Apart from saying Mass then, what does a priest do which is priestly? Well he can visit his people. If he's an earnest priest he may indeed visit his people. Perhaps two hundred homes for half an hour each year. Given a good programme, well advertised, and a good slot of the evening, we can visit half a million homes for half an hour in one evening.

My tendency and attitude always has been to reject the strict division that some make between laymen and priests, as if they were different species of Homo Sapiens. Every priest is, after all, a layman until he is ordained at the quarter century.

I have seen large areas in different parts of the world where all the functions of a priest except hearing Confessions and saying Mass are performed by laymen and women. By every human measurement they are as good and effective if not better and more effective than ordained priests. Doesn't the priest lead his people in prayer? Apart from the Holy Eucharist, most priests that I know have no particular charism to inspire people to prayer. Some have, but so also do some lay men and women. The ability to pray and to lead others in prayer is no respector of the Sacrament of Orders.

My instinct is to cut through vague talk of what is a priest's job and what isn't. And to look at the question in an existentialist fashion.

A priest has six or more years training in philosophy and theology. By the fact of accepting this particular vocation in the Church and remaining celibate, the priest is relatively freer to work in the cause of Christ and his Church. I don't think he is necessarily more committed than his lay sisters and brethren. But he may have a lot less commitments.

Because a priest has intellectual training in the things of God, and because he has the commitment and time to work in the cause of God, then it seems to me not unreasonable that he be associated with the talk about God in radio and television.

Television needs people who are committed to a certain area of interest be it sport, or current affairs, or agriculture, and who are willing and able to give it their all.

Broadcasting is a very demanding area to work in. Many of the more successful men and women working in broadcasting are either single, or if they are not single, are prone to neglect their family.

I am not saying that priests should take over religious

121

broadcasting. Far from it. But it should not be thought extraordinary for them to make a contribution.

So, for me the idea of priests working in media is normal and natural, and should need no defence or justification. However, in practice, a priest working in media is questioned from right and left.

I am the new not-afraid-to-talk-to-young-people TV priest!

I am quite certain that some journalists whom I admire and respect, feel suspicious or even resentful of a priest working in media. Part of this is the fear that the priest may not be entirely free, that he may be manipulated from on high in the interest of increased clerical control.

On the other side, most bishops and many lower clergy consider a priest working in television to be merely indulging a hobby — the true priest is engaged in *pastoral* work (pastoral from the latin word 'pastor', meaning a shepherd), although it is never very clear what this actually embraces.

For my part I think the word 'pastoral' might be better dropped, and the word 'shepherd' be reserved for the Good Shepherd Himself. The cleric who identifies himself with the role of shepherd may well come to think of the laity as sheep: the two images can't easily be separated.

And sheep seems to me an inappropriate image for the laity in the light of much that was said and written about them at Vatican II.

122

The significance of media revolutions
I think that a reasonable case was made by the late Marshall McLuhan for the view that the great turning points in human history were not occasioned by philosophers or even generals, but by changes in the way men speak to each other.

The last great turning point in the history of communications, the invention of printing, was also a turning point in the history of religion. This was not a coincidence. The invention of printing not only made it possible for the ideas of the Protestant Reformation to become widespread. It provided the stimulus for these ideas in the first place.

With the relatively recent introduction of radio and television, we are in the middle of another media revolution comparable to the invention of printing.

It may be too early to measure its full significance. But this does not prevent us from looking at what happened the last time, and seeing what can be learnt.

Printing and the Protestant Reformation
If you wanted to make a copy of the Book of Kells nowadays and had the skilled artists and craftsmen to prepare the material, write the words and illustrate the page, the cost would be in six figures.

The book is written on vellum made from animal skin. The vellum for three hundred and forty pages could cost over £40,000 for a start. The actual writing of the text, with minor illuminations would take about five thousand hours according to one estimate. At £10 an hour that's £50,000. Then there are the forty illuminated pages . . . It is not difficult to see why books were rare before printing.

Only two groups had access to books before printing: the very rich, who could afford to collect them, and the clerics who made books themselves and gathered them over centuries in libraries to which only they had access. (cf *The Name of the Rose.*) Apart from the clerics who had to read the Office and Mass, there was little incentive for anybody else to learn to read, since there was nothing available to read anyway.

In those days, which lasted up to the era of Gutenberg and Caxton, people learned of God and what the Bible said about him from the spoken word. They listened to the cleric, the only one in the community with access to God's word and the wisdom of the ages. This was the era of the clerical Church par excellence, where the cleric was a necessary medium for handing on the faith.

123

He's trained to bring in a chapter at a time!

Being the only ones with access to the word of God in the Bible, the cleric was in an extremely powerful position to preserve the unity of the church in a formal outward sense: to decide what people must or must not believe.

So the invention of printing posed an enormous threat to the clerical Church. It meant for the first time that the clerics could not have complete control over religious thought and practice. For the first time, the Bible could be made in sufficient copies to make it worthwhile for people to learn to read and to study it for themselves without the felt need of a priest to mediate the message. They could go away into a corner and read and reflect for themselves.

It was printing that made private reading possible, and hence also private interpretation and private judgement. It is clear now that the official Church had no understanding of what was happening. The scholastic theologians considered the printing press a toy and the vernacular booklet as a play-thing for the peasant. And in a lot of learned debates in the crypts of cathedrals, they refuted in latin the arguments of the heretics, unaware that the real battles were being fought and lost elsewhere.

But if the Church didn't change, many of the laity and some

of the lower clergy changed so much that they no longer felt that the Church they knew was relevant enough to justify maintaining formal unity. They wanted to read the Bible; to pray in their own language, not latin; and believe, hope and love God with greater freedom. And if they couldn't have that in the Roman Catholic Church, they would leave.

Far from seeing the tremendous benefit to mankind, and the enormous opportunities offered by the print medium for the development of religion and the wider understanding of the Gospel, the Church tried to stem the tide. People were forbidden to read the Bible in their own language. Those who would not obey were subject to the traditional sanctions, which however effective in the past, now only helped to speed-up and confirm the break-up of Christianity.

It took a long time for the Catholic Church to learn its mistake. The Second Vatican Council may be seen as one of the last steps it took to adapt – after five hundred years – to the invention of printing. In the declaration of religious freedom, the acceptance of the vernacular in the liturgy, and the stress laid on the Bible in the spiritual life of the ordinary Christian, the Church took on board again, after five hundred years, three of the main planks of the Protestant Reformation.

Will it take another five hundred years to catch up this time?

The Broadcasting Revolution
I could easily write pages on how I think the Church is failing to adapt to the latest media revolution. I could draw up a list of the mistakes the Church is currently making. And how in the long run it is going to have to pay for them. But I won't, because every statement, in the nature of things, could be contested. And the people one might wish to convince will find enough to disagree with to miss the wood for the trees. So I will stick to one observation.

If it can be accepted now that significant media change such as the advent of printing, and now radio and television, can bring about substantial changes in society, then an institution like the Catholic Church, which is essentially an institution for communicating a message, should stay close to the action, and make every effort to understand what's happening. That is the theory. Now what is the Irish reality?

Well, the Catholic Church's media training centre has recently been leased for five years to RTÉ. After the first few years, few if any diocesan priests were sent for serious training there. The facilities were used mostly by people from the Third World.

In a diocese with about five hundred secular priests, and one thousand religious, it appears that no younger priest can be made available to ensure the continuation of a project like Radharc.

18

Freelancing

In 1975 I suggested a radical approach to Irish broadcasting in a two-part article in the *Irish Times*. Among other things I proposed that RTÉ be broken up into two independent channels with distinct areas of special interest, in competition for viewers, but sharing transmitters and certain other facilities. The radical approach was never adopted, but some of the comments on free-lancing may be worth re-quoting.

"The independent second channel should also tap the mostly untapped resources of free-lance programming. Free-lancers provide their own buildings, services and equipment. Programmes are produced without capital expenditure from public funds. Payment is by results. Opportunities are created for the development of broadcasting talent which are not so easy to come by in a monolithic set-up . . .

Two objections to free-lancing programming are sometimes advanced: lack of quality and lack of editorial control.

With regard to lack of quality, the free-lancer who produces a poor product will go out of business very quickly, which is no problem for anyone except himself. With regard to control, a programme controller is likely to have on average more control over free-lance programmes than directly originated output, much of which he can't even see before it is broadcast. If there is a danger in free-lancing, it might lie in a diminution of the creative freedom of the producer – do what I say or go out of business.

There is a frustration in Irish broadcasting at present. Creative people want to make more programmes and better programmes, and the whole system seems at times to work against them.

They are caught in a tradition and a system which most have not cared to criticise, and nobody seems able to break, but which is beginning to have a crippling effect.

One of the tools of trade unions in protecting people's jobs is to lay down lines of demarcation. But it is a tool – a means to an end. Sometimes in changed circumstances the means have to be changed to reach the same end. It is my feeling that this is now beginning to be true of broadcasting in Ireland.

I think it is time that management in RTÉ took another look at priorities – hopefully to decide that broadcasting is about programmes rather than prestigious plant and engineering. Time too that unions got together with management to consider how they might increase the creative opportunities and job satisfaction of their members, and to adopt a more flexible approach to what in the present critical situation are lesser problems – whose right it is to move a chair or put in a bulb.''

There has been a lot of progress since 1975 when this was written. The big success story in broadcasting in recent years has been Channel 4. Based on new thinking in the Annan Report on the Future of Broadcasting (1977), it was set up amidst some opposition and much prophesying of doom and early death. In fact, it has not only survived, it is a financial and cultural success.

Its programmes are different, exciting, and often break new ground. The success of Channel 4 has made free-lancing, in these islands anyway, not only legitimate but fashionable. But it wasn't always so.

I remember many years ago that some of the best people in British broadcasting put their heads together, left the BBC and set up an independent production company. Ludovic Kennedy was one of the leaders who is still around.

The programmes were magnificent and nobody disputed the fact. But they couldn't sell them. The BBC were unwilling to cede control of content to any outside group. What programmes were shown on ITV were shown at bad times. So the group folded up and the members drifted back to working as individuals for their old masters.

When consultants were brought in to RTÉ in 1985, one of their recommendations was to increase the quotient of free-lance programming. The result was that attractive packages are now being offered to staff to encourage them to go out on their own, including guarantees to take at least part of their output.

It is never easy to give up a steady job and pension, and go out and live on your wits, especially if you have a wife and family. But some are doing it.

A number of people who worked with Radharc have gone on to work with RTÉ. One thing they all miss is the freedom associated with independent production. Working for Radharc, Brian O'Reilly used to shoot all the film. Then he used to edit all the film. At other times he built electronic equipment, prepared graphic material, and produced animated film sequences. After fourteen years he went to RTÉ where he held the job of film editor and later cameraman, in turn, not together. But he got bored and went to Australia where I am told he has a production unit of his own.

Brian was good enough to get a job in RTÉ at any time. If he stayed with Radharc for fourteen years it can only be because he relished the freedom and variety of the work, which he knew he couldn't expect in a large organisation.

19

Finance and Organisation

After the first two programmes appeared, RTÉ sent us a cheque for £64. I sent it back, saying it wasn't worth cashing.

In 1962 and 1963 we were paid £125 per programme — about £1,100 in present money. This had to cover film stock, processing, travel expenses and any overheads. In 1964 the payment improved to £250 per programme with travel expenses within Ireland at current RTÉ rates.

In its first few years, Radharc only survived because the priests involved paid their own travel and accommodation expenses and took no honorarium or salary.

The Archbishop of Dublin provided the cash for the first camera owned by Radharc. However, this was considered to be an interest-free loan and eventually paid back to the diocese.

In addition to the stipend from RTÉ – always the main source of income – there have always been two other sources. Radharc has rights to the use of programmes outside television. In the past, the sale of programmes on film was an important factor. But nowadays people want videos not films, and while the volume is higher the actual profit per video is so small that it doesn't compensate. The third source of income is commissions from religious or development groups like Gorta or Trócaire who may want a film produced for their own purposes. Depending on type or content, this may or may not be offered to television. We never take commissions from commercial sources. In recent years a little programming for Channel 4 has provided useful extra income.

Radharc has always been paid less per programme than other freelance producers. This may be because we never pressed to be paid more, or it may be that RTÉ mistakenly presumed we had other secret sources of income. However, I was a little shaken early in the eighties to learn about another freelance producer who was pressing RTÉ to increase his programme fee which he considered totally uneconomic. For the first time ever, I enquired what another freelancer was currently receiving. It was two and a half times our stipend. We were doing programmes all over the world paying our own travel expenses, whereas the other producer confined his work to Ireland and England. We were also carrying an overdraft which touched £30,000. Our fee was increased by 25% that year. We can stay out of the red some of the time now, provided we don't employ many people. But it still isn't easy.

In fairness to RTÉ it should be said that the total amount paid to Radharc is probably not less than that paid to some other freelance producers. In recent years, Radharc production has been fifteen half-hour programmes per year, which is a higher production rate than other free-lancers are currently attempting. There were periods when Radharc only produced five programmes a year, but in my opinion this level of production would not justify the full-time involvement of a priest.

One key to Radharc's financial survival of course has been the practice continued from the beginning, with some exceptions, that priests who contribute to Radharc receive no salary or fee.

131

Travel expenses are also lower because we tend to stay in religious houses in foreign countries. We can also avail of certain discounts for missionary travel, although these are small. Where other freelancers are concerned, or skilled staff, we pay the going rates.

Legal status

When Radharc began, the Dublin Diocese was unwilling to take legal responsibility lest someone might bring a libel action as a result of a programme indiscretion, and take the Diocese to the cleaners. For a long time therefore, the position remained anomalous. Legal advisors eventually concluded that Radharc was a partnership owned by Des Forristal and myself. When I returned to fulltime direction in the seventies Des assigned his share to me, and I arranged with the cooperation of the Revenue Commissioners to turn Radharc into a charitable trust.

Independence

Throughout twenty-five years, the independence of Radharc has been respected totally by the Irish Church.

Priests or Religious who work for Radharc, do so with the permission of their bishop or superior. But after that, they are responsible to the Director of Radharc for their work in film. Appointments to Radharc are made by the Director.

The only interference by Archbishop John Charles, who was considered to be a very interfering bishop, was to suggest two subjects for programmes, and give out about another. (See Chapter 3).

I have no record or memory of interference by either of his successors.

Bias

A critic once wrote of one of our programmes that it would have been different if it hadn't been made by a priest.

My answer to that was, "Yes. So what?" Every programme is biased because it is directed by a human being who has a certain background and prejudices. It is only a fool who thinks otherwise. If the programme maker is responsible, he tries not to let his biases interfere too much. That is all that is humanly possible.

Sure I am biased. I am against the use of atomic energy in any form. I am for J.S. Bach. I am against the music business because it prejudices people against J.S.Bach because J.S. Bach won't make them enough money. I am for capitalism I think, because my father

132

was a shopkeeper and I haven't yet seen socialism work very well in the long-term. (It's too much like Christianity — expects everybody to be saints, and they aren't.) I am a conscientious objector if such things exist anymore, and wouldn't ever shoot a bird or a rabbit. I am anti-English and anti-Spanish because of what they did in their colonies. I generally support one political party which I am too cute to tell you about. And I am for Jesus Christ.

Let the next man speak for himself.

20

RTÉ and the viewing Public

Relationships with RTÉ are based on goodwill and trust. Radharc proposes a list of subjects each year which are discussed with the Programme Controller or his representative. However, a great measure of freedom is allowed because opportunities may appear in the field which are too good to miss.

This particularly applies to overseas work. RTÉ takes the responsibility for broadcasting and therefore has the right to reject material at any stage. This only happened once. The year was 1964 and the topic was discrimination against Catholics in Derry. The subject was cleared with Jack White, Assistant Programme Controller, and the filming completed. The situation in Derry was one of gerrymandering and injustice and it certainly moved us to anger at the time. When we returned and had processed and part-edited the material, the Programme Controller, Gunnar Rugheimer said he would prefer not to broadcast the material. This was the period of the Lemass/O'Neill meetings, and RTÉ didn't wish to do anything which might rock the boat. We were disappointed but anxious at the same time to be seen to accept the Controller's authority in such matters without question.

The film included interviews with Brian Friel's father, and other notables of the time, which might be interesting to look back on today. But there's one thing it didn't have which would have made it even more interesting. People at the time said that it was a pity we had missed a bright young man who would have had something to say to us, but was unfortunately out of Derry at the time. His name was John Hume.

I only once dug in my heels with RTÉ. It was decided at Programme Controller level, or maybe even higher, that Radharc should come under the Religion Department. I opposed this tooth and nail. I fought with Gunnar Rugheimer, Programme Controller — as many other people did — and later with the Director General Kevin McCourt who pressed my arm hard. So much so that I had to play the ultimate card. I said that if we had to come under the Religious Programmes Department, then we would no longer be interested in making programmes.

I could give several bad reasons why I wanted to stay clear of the Religion Department. But there's one reason which is enough to make me thankful that we fought this one out. If we had come under the Religion Department, then we would have been beholden to them for money — money out of their budget, money which they might well feel would have been better used by themselves. (The department has always been short of money.) A second lesser reason is that we would have been at one remove from the seat of power and decision-making, the Programme Controller.

The position at the beginning, which remains today, is that Radharc is responsible to the Programme Controller, and is budgeted for separately. And so may it remain.

Because we may need services, help, advice, or simply to exchange information, we've always had relationships at all different levels with RTÉ. These have tended to become closer relationships as the years go by. Many nowadays might be better termed friendships. So when we have a problem, we know who in RTÉ to phone to help us sort it out. Certain functions in the production process, notably film dubbing which we used to do outside, we now do in RTÉ. We seem invariably to get the kind of help which we have no right to expect but for which we are the more grateful.

In former years I tended to keep a distance from RTÉ, largely because I felt that this was the way that RTÉ would wish it to be. One of the advantages of freelancers is that they deliver completed programmes without the need for the broadcasting organisation to get too much involved.

But there probably was another reason as well — the fear of meeting rejection from some who might resent our freedom of action and somewhat unorthodox methods of producing programmes. After twenty-five years and two hundred and fifty programmes one worries less about such things. Radharc is a little part of RTÉ's history, and nothing can ever change that.

Public acceptance
We used to employ a press cutting agency up to some time in the early seventies but money then got scarcer than usual so we gave it up.

Looking back on those old cuttings today I can only say with more truth than humility, that I am surprised. We couldn't have read them at the time or we would have got swelled heads!

Radharc, the most distinctive and distinguished series of programmes devised for Telefís Éireann in its two year history. — *Irish Press.*

Radharc impresses me as a first rate magazine programme. And would that it's sharp pictorial clarity and its eye for composition were the rule rather than the exception. — *Munster Tribune*

Radharc in my opinion is the most competently produced home programme on Telefís. — *Irish Catholic*

I have nothing but the sincerest admiration for the Radharc team's work. — *Irish Times*

Nor can I close another week without another, (yes yet another) word of praise for Radharc. — *Evening Herald*

Once again Radharc evidenced the inventiveness and interviewing skill that marked out the series for the Jacobs award. — *Irish Independent*

It was a superb film. — *Sunday Independent*

The number of cuttings was another surprise. These days if we get one or two mentions we are pleased. One programme in 1968 spawned at least forty-four press notices.

What did we have that earned us such notices? At a time when RTÉ was struggling to get a basic service going, they had to work mostly out of studios in Dublin. We were free to roam the country.

We didn't have to work to the same deadline pressure. We offered things when we felt they were ready.

For a while in the beginning it was possible to keep one jump ahead; we were the first team for instance to travel abroad on behalf of RTÉ; to England first, and then further afield.

But there were other factors perhaps. I think Peter Lemass was a better interviewer than he may have got credit for (the BBC once offered him a job). I think Des Forristal's ability to see what is important in a story, his skill in organising the available material

136

and his crisp scriptwriting left the stamp of a good mind on the programmes.

There may also have been an element of fresh fun. A group of friends going off on holiday together and making films. Perhaps some of the enjoyment of making them came through to the programmes themselves.

At the ten year mark we were still doing well. In 1971, every one of seven programmes in a row appeared in the RTÉ top ten.

The first one was 8th in the ratings. The second was 1st — ahead of *The Dubliners* and the *Late Late Show*. Next time round it was 6th — ahead of the *Riordans,* the then equivalent of *Glenroe.* After that it was 3rd, 7th, 6th, and lastly 2nd (to the *Late Late*).

And what is the situation today? Well it is difficult to make comparisons when there has been so much change. Most of the country *had* to watch RTÉ in 1971. Now we have multi-channel TV, which not only divides the audience, but puts pressure on schedule planners to keep peak viewing hours for entertainment. We still get good positions in the programme schedules, but of course nothing like the favoured slots the programmes once enjoyed.

But one thing is at least certain. It is a long time since Radharc appeared in the top ten! A spot check with Audience Measurement indicates that the average audience for each of the last four programmes produced by Radharc in 1985 was half a million.

And what do the critics say nowadays? We were filming outside Dublin a few days ago, when a lady we interviewed took a local newspaper out of the coal bucket to show us the television column. The big print said,

"The excellent Radharc series came up trumps again . . ."

Such superlatives aren't common. But there is still enough positive comment to encourage one to continue making programmes. Like the prophets, we possibly get more kudos abroad. Radharc has won five international awards: given the fact that these awards are only made every second or third year, this is not a bad record, and is probably only beaten by the British and the Dutch.

A second bite of the cherry
Within the past year a new priest was appointed to Peter Lemass's parish in Chile, a Columban who used to be in charge of mission promotion in Australia. The new priest was talking to a third person about the Mercy Sisters in Argentina, when Peter was present.

After a little while Peter realised that he was talking about a film in which Peter had been involved as scriptwriter and interviewer. "You seem to know more about that film than I do," said Peter. "Well, I ought to," said the Columban, "I've seen it over eighty times."

The Society for the Propagation of the Faith in England get a new Radharc film every year. They use it as an introduction to talks around the country on mission. At the end of the year it goes into library stock and they buy another.

Over a period of four years, 1979 to 1983, three hundred and sixty films were sold for educational use. These were bought by such diverse organisations as the Open University, the Scottish Health Education Bureau, Villa Nova University in the United States, and the Jesuit Curia.

Now that so many people have video players, the market for film is very much reduced. This has meant a cut into what used to be an important source of income for Radharc. By the time one takes off VAT, the cost of tape, transfer, printing and publicity, there is little to be made from a video. The only answer is quantity, but this means commercial marketing which is a very different operation to film making.

We would be happy to get the films and the name around in greater quantities, even if there wasn't much revenue. But so far, we've only been dabbling.

21

Looking Forward

Now that the first twenty five years are over, what about the next?

Television changes; but there is still likely to be a place for all the usual things like news and sport and documentary and religion.

I hope Radharc can continue to make a worthwhile contribution, and I hope RTÉ will continue to want us to try.

With regard to myself, I still retain the original interest and enthusiasm: I can still keep going longer and harder in the field than most younger men. Good health of course is the controlling factor. One can only presume it may continue until there are contrary indications, otherwise one would never do anything. My grandfather retired at sixty and died at one hundred and four.

Having "taken the shilling", I could of course be forbidden to continue. But I hope not. I am probably safer making little films than out in some big parochial house where I might find more time to write scurrilous articles and books! (This one has cost me five programmes at least).

I would very much like to involve more younger people in Radharc, and of course I try. The average age of the team that worked recently on programmes in America (excluding me) was twenty-five.

They were laymen. I would like one or two priests or sisters from the next generation as well. Over the last five years I have made efforts, using younger priests on their holidays at home and abroad, letting them find out what the work involved and letting me learn something of what they are capable of. It's an expensive business trying out people, and time-consuming. I have asked at one time or another for some one of them to be released to work with Radharc for a year to learn the business. Once I was promised action, but no action followed. Another time the request was met with silence.

The problem is that any priest who would be useful to Radharc would also be able to do a lot of other things which have a higher pastoral (that word again!) priority. On the part of a clever young man who is also ambitious there could be another problem. Working in media does not confer social status, as would an academic post. Nor does it help one on the way to ecclesiastical honours — quite the contrary.

Years and years ago we used to have arguments every now and then at production meetings about whether we should be making programmes at all. I felt then that we should. I still feel the same way.

Well speaking as a moron, I enjoyed it.

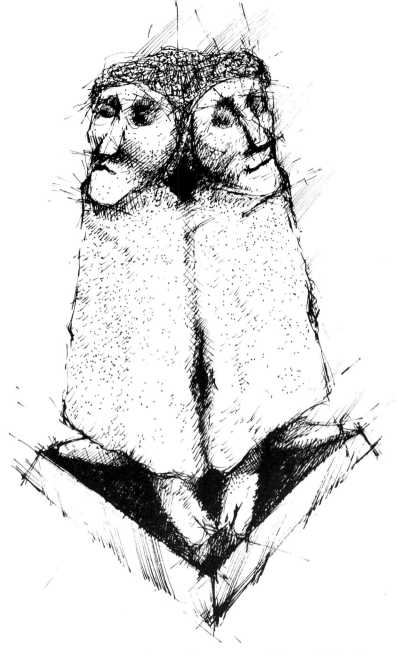

Radharc — Al O'Donnell . 14/1/86

The new *Radharc* logo.
Designed by Al O'Donnell.
Sculpted by Niall O'Neill.

141

People who work(ed) for Radharc

Byrne, Philip
Film Editor. Now Manager, Quality Assurance Unit, AnCO.

Caffrey, Jim
Presented six programmes, five in the Far East. Now CC Meadowbrook, Dublin.

Canning, Peter
Film Editor. Now producer in RTÉ.

Carey, Pat
Sound Technician. Now bank official.

Cassidy, Eoin
Scripted and presented two programmes.

Connaughton, Dáithí
Sound Technician. Now Film Editor, RTÉ.

Cross, Raymond
Sound Technician. Now freelance.

Daly, Martin
Presented seven programmes. Now CC Navan Rd.

Doran, Dáibhí
Film Editor. Now freelance. Has edited over forty Radharcs.

Dunn, Joseph
Director of Radharc.

Dunne, Sean
Columban film maker. Now edits *The Far East*.

Durham, Keith
Sound Technician. Now freelance assistant cameraman.

Fitzgerald, William
Played a variety of roles. Now Head of Religious Programmes, RTÉ.

Flavin, Donal
Helped with equipment and lighting in the early days. Died 1968.

Flood, Sheila
Secretary. Now Secretary, the Communications Centre.

Foley, Michael
Sound Technician. Now executive in the AV Dept, UCD.

Forristal, Desmond
Former Director, scriptwriter of many films. Now PP Dalkey.

Gaughran, Roseanna
Secretarial assistant.

Kelly, Peter
Current staff. Assistant Producer, editor.

Lemass, Peter
Main interviewer. Also writes scripts. Currently working in Chile.

Madden, John
Current Staff. Sound Technician.

McCarthy, Dermod
Unit Manager and director of many films. Now Administrator Pro Cathedral.

Ó Fiaich, Tomás Cardinal
Presented five programmes on historical subjects.

O'Keeffe, Con
Researcher for most of the early programmes. Now PP Bohernabreena.

O'Laoghaire, Art
Sound Technician. Now freelance.

O'Reilly, Anne
Current staff. Management and secretarial.

O'Reilly, Brian
Cameraman, editor and general factotum for fourteen years. Now in Australia.

O'Rinn, Liam
Film Editor. Now Film Editor, RTÉ.

Sheehy, Maureen
Researcher, Scriptwriter.

Stack, Tom
Scriptwriter and interviewer, CC Donnybrook.

Swords, Liam
Researcher and Director of history programmes. Now Proviseur, Irish College, Paris.

Turley, Darach
Director and Scriptwriter.

Appendix 2

A complete list of Radharc films

Asterisk denotes approximate time.
Other timings correct to nearest second.
Tx = *Date of first transmission*

Ireland/UK

1   Croagh Patrick
    The Sodality
    The Mass Rock.
    Time: 26.40.* Tx 12.1.62

2   The New Ritual
    Glenties and the Tidy Towns
    The Irish College *Ranafast*
    Time: 26.40.* Tx 9.2.62

3   Blessing the Aer Lingus fleet
    Lough Derg, Penal Crosses
    Manners in Church
    Time: 26.40.* Tx 15.9.62

4   Convent vocations
    Preparing for a Sick Call
    Stamps for the Missions
    The Story of Lourdes
    Time: 26.40.* Tx 4.10.62

5   Sunshine House
    The Story of Christy Brown
    Time: 26.40. Tx 18.10.62

6   Tax on Kerry Cows
    Retreat House, Raheny
    Kylemore Abbey
    Time: 26.40.* Tx 8.11.62

7   Christian Symbolism
    Services for Emigrants
    Poaching and Poachers
    Time: 26.40.* Tx 21.11.62

8   Ballintubber Abbey
    Thanks after Communion
    The Small Farmer
    Time: 26.40.* Tx 13.12.62

9   The Young Offender
    The first film in an Irish prison
    Time: 29.30. Tx 12.9.63

The first Jacobs Award, which Radharc received as 'the most enterprising programme on Irish TV'. Being cute we re-presented it to John Charles, and it remained in his office for the duration of his reign. His successor returned it in the general tidy up.

10   The Twelve Apostles
     The Churching of Women
     Columban Martyrs in Korea
     Time: 26.59. Tx 26.9.63

11   The Black Valley Church
     The Station Mass
     Time: 26.40. Tx 10.10.63

12   Irish Summer Holidays
     Traditional Prayers
     The Kenmare Weather Cock
     Time: 26.40.* Tx 17.10.63

13   Religious Stamp Collecting
     Tourism brings life to Kerry
     Time: 26.40.* Tx 7.11.63

14   Honesty at the Fair
     Is there an honest man at an
     Irish fair?
     Time: 26.40.* Tx 21.11.63

14a Fr Casey and the Land War
     Eyewitness account of land war
     Time: 27.35. Tx 5.12.63

15   The Bell and the Ark
     Stories from Clare
     Fr Theobald Matthew
     Time: 27.32. Tx 19.12.63

16   We knew Matt Talbot
     People who worked with Matt
     Time: 60.22. Tx 25.3.64

17   Down and Out in Dublin
     Frank speaking by gentlemen of
     the road
     Time: 26.38. Tx 1.11.64

18   Catholic Enquiry Centre
     Community Development
     Armagh
     Time: 26.18. Tx 29.11.64

19   Hotel Chaplain
     Mission to Irish in Britain
     Time: 26.26. Tx 10.1.65

20   Oldbury Camp
     Chaplain to building site
     Time: 26.40. Tx 14.2.65

21   House Hunters
     Fr Casey's Housing Aid Society
     Time: 26.40.* Tx 28.2.65

22   The Boat Train to Euston
     Graiguenamanagh Abbey
     Time: 26.40. Tx 21.3.65

The team filming at Dublin Airport in 1962. L to R: Self, Sean Dunne, Peter Lemass,
Billy Fitzgerald, Donal Flavin.

144

"That thing isn't switched on, is it?" The Young Offender *was probably the first documentary ever made in an Irish prison.*

145

The first trip abroad was to film aspects of the work of emigrant chaplains in England. Oldbury Camp, 1965, was about the work of the chaplain to a building site.

146

John Charles, whom De Valera had asked the Vatican to appoint as Archbishop of Dublin. Behind, L to R: William Cardinal Conway and Self.

147

148

Dermod McCarthy holds UNDA WACC trophy awarded to Heirs of the Father, *which he directed, and Des Forristal (left) scripted.*

149

Nano, *a dramatised documentary on the foundress of the Presentation Order.*

Europe

Father Borelli's street gang in Naples. At the time the photo was taken, the others were unaware that Borelli, second from left, was a priest.

151

Cardinal Tomás Ó Fiaich waits patiently while incompetent director tries to make up his mind what to do next. St Gall, City and Saint, *1982.*

152

*The Radharc Team in Arizona 1985. L to R: John Madden, Peter Kelly, Darach Turley
and Self. Note much favoured location.*

153

Rose Kennedy is a real professional. Between hairdo, make-up and floral arrangements, it took about three hours to prepare for the interview. Mother of the Kennedys, *1973.*

154

Archbishop Helder Camara and friend with, behind, L to R: Brian O'Reilly, Dermod McCarthy, Dáithí Connaughton and Tom Stack. The Earth Belongs to Everyone, *1977.*

South America

155

The old style missionary. Padre Joao is a Kerryman, *1977.*

How cameramen get bilharziasis. And if you don't know what that is, look up a medical dictionary and thank God for influenza.

156

An historic photo. Jomo Kenyatta, first President of Kenya, flanked on his left by his wife and her brother, a priest of the diocese of Nairobi, and on his right by his father-in-law, Chief Mohoho and some of his thirteen wives and innumerable children. Kikuyu Country, *1966.*

The Cessna which brought us around Kenya in 1965.

157

*An Irish Round Tower in Sierra Leone.
Built of stone by a homesick missionary.
No doubt the Africans will find it
useful when the Vikings come.*

158

Des Forristal with group of admirers on the shores of Lake Rudolf. Gorta Gives a Dam, *1973.*

A Turkana tribesman with feathered mudcap, spear, and headrest. Turkana, *1966.*

Mrs Sweeney's people came to Montserrat in the West Indies in Cromwellian times. When she went to the US some years ago, she passed herself off as Irish, which she found a much more helpful label than 'West Indian'. The Black Irish, 1976.

Oscar Arnulfo Romero, Archbishop of San Salvador was shot while holding up the chalice at the Consecration of the Mass. Interviewed in Who is for Liberation? *1980.*

Fidel Castro looking less than comfortable in the pulpit of a Havana church — the first time he had been in a church for 25 years. Here there is no Christmas, *1986*.

A Guatemalan woman of Mayan stock consoles her baby. Where the Pope is a Communist, *1984*.

Asia

*"Somebody tell them to cut the cackle — the insects are killing me." Brian O'Reilly,
Bede Griffith, and Self.* Krishna and Christ, *1977.*

The Restless Knives, *1968, a film about the sugar workers in the Philippines was made with the help of a very young Niall O'Brien, who later achieved fame by being imprisoned. The film won an UNDA award, and was shown extensively abroad. A Dutch TV Director told me within the last year that it was a seminal film which influenced them at the time of their approach to religious documentary.*

L to R: Brian O'Reilly, Neville Presho and glum Indian Information Officer brought back from his holidays to watch us film cows. Gorta in India, *1977*.

165

"No. But my father was very fond of missionaries." Billy Fitzgerald, Dermod McCarthy with camera, and friend. Wantok, *1974*.